Decorating Country Style

A Complete Guide to Paint Effects and Stencilling

BETTERWAY BOOKS
Cincinnati, OH

Decorating Country Style. Copyright © 2000 by Betterway Books. Manufactured in China. All rights reserved. The patterns in this book are for the personal use of the reader. By permission of the publisher, they may be hand-traced or photocopied to make single copies, but under no circumstances may they be resold or republished. No other part of this book may be reproduced in any form or by any electronic or mechanical means including information storage and retrieval systems without permission in writing from the publisher, except by a reviewer, who may quote brief passages in a review. Published by Betterway Books, an imprint of F&W Publications, Inc., 1507 Dana Avenue, Cincinnati, Ohio 45207. (800) 289-0963. First edition.

Visit our Web site at www.artistsnetwork.com for information on more resources for artists.

04 03 02 01 00   5 4 3 2 1

A catalog record for this book is available from the U.S. Library of Congress.

ISBN 1-55870-574-0

Editorial Production Manager: Kathi Howard
Production Coordinator: Sara Dumford
Studio Manager: Ruth Preston

Contents

❧❧❧

CHAPTER 1

Creating a Country Look

AMERICAN country style

The warm and welcoming style that was established by the American colonists was simple and practical—and endures as one of today's most popular ways of decorating the home.

Painted furniture

Although time has muted the original colors associated with the American country style, those hues—especially reds—were once rich and highly saturated. To create the look of antique painted finishes on today's furniture, add simple painted motifs for visual interest, then rub paint in spots to simulate wear.

The style that has come to be known as American country is rooted in our pioneer past but was truly reborn as a legacy of the Bicentennial of 1976. The last 20 years have witnessed a burgeoning and refining of this hugely popular style.

When the earliest colonists landed in New England and Virginia, they brought virtually nothing with them but their courage and ingenuity. What they encountered was a densely forested wilderness. The forest offered an abundance of wood, a material thankfully familiar to them. The dwelling places these settlers assembled were crude single-room cabins, and their furnishings were elemental, comprising a motley array of hand-hewn stools, benches, sawbuck tables and cradles, plus a handful of basic necessities, such as drinking vessels and serving pieces called *trenchers* that often had to double as dinnerware. Virtually everything was crafted of wood. Joinery was precise and sturdy; dovetails and pegs mark early rustic pieces.

As transatlantic crossings increased and

Shaker style

The Shakers, a religious sect that flourished in the late 19th century, are renowned for their spartan approach to design. Built-in storage, room-girdling pegboard and a marine blue-green they favored speak to the style.

Printed fabrics

Once fabrics could be mass-produced by machine, there was much more latitude for creating patterns and prints. Mixing prints is one way to enliven a country room; florals and gingham checks, for example, coordinate wonderfully.

Country accents

■ Due to the scarcity of glass, windows in early houses tended to be small with multiple panes. Walls were thick, so windows were set into deep recesses fitted with internal shutters. As windows became larger, shutters gave way to fabric treatments. In the South, shutters endured; they repelled the sun while admitting breezes into a room.

■ When dressing a country window, steer away from fussy treatments. Roller blinds, a simple swag or a pair of tab-top curtains work best. Keep fabrics simple, too. Checks, stripes, tickings or florals set the right mood.

■ Before central heating, many rooms had a fireplace, and it became the focal point of the room. Fireplace walls might exhibit chimneypieces or paneling; pieces of art might hang over fireplace mantels. Many early paintings, such as theorems, stencil-like still lifes, are naive in appearance. Prints of such paintings are not hard to find.

■ Like the Shakers, the Amish were a sect that evolved an aesthetic based on a lack of ornament. Because of their craftsmanship, Amish quilts—worked in deep jewel tones— are highly prized.

America's population and fortunes grew, so did a ready supply of more varied materials. Furniture and pattern books imported from abroad inspired cabinetmakers to replicate or adapt favorite pieces that suited the larger homes of the emerging bourgeoisie. Even so, almost everything still had to be made by hand—including nails and fittings, though these now could be forged of iron.

Functional furniture

Much early furniture was designed to be not only functional but multifunctional. When a single space, such as a keeping room, had to harbor a variety of activities such as cooking, eating and sleeping, flexibility was key. Thus tilt-back settles converted to tables and hatchback tables to chairs. Blanket chests provided seating. Notched candlestands could be adjusted to the height of a burning candle. And early beds were lashed together with rope so they could be taken apart and moved as necessary.

As cabinetry skills increased, furniture elements began to be turned on the lathe, not merely cut and planed. Chair shapes, for example, grew more complex. Ladder-backs, splint backs and Windsors are time-honored designs that have become classics of the American country genre.

Homespun fabrics

Like their hand-hewn counterparts in furniture, early fabrics had to be woven by hand. Called homespuns because they were, in fact, woven at home, early textiles—plainspoken linens and woolens (and, later, cottons)—were left unbleached or tinted with dyes extracted from plants. Indigo was a popular hue, as were mustard yellow, various shades of brown and the ruddy tone we now call barn red. Because of the plain over/under configuration of the linen weave, fabric designs tended to play on uncomplicated stripes and checks. Later, crewelwork and other needlework techniques, such as red "turkeywork" and tatting, were employed to embellish textiles.

Early Americans were, of necessity, thrifty and recycled everything. Scraps of precious cloth were restitched into patchwork quilts. The American quilt, an indigenous craft, evolved into an art form and is now considered an icon of the American country style.

Walls and floors

Surfaces in the home—walls, floors and ceilings—were often left in their natural state. Because wallpapers were imported, they were prohibitively expensive. To simulate their effect, itinerant muralists were retained to paint scenic views on walls. Stencils, too, were an attractive and affordable alternative, whether used for borders or allover designs. Popular designs included the pineapple, the symbol of hospitality; the fleur-de-lis; and leaves and vines.

Floors tended to be planed smooth and left bare. Wealthier Americans imported Oriental rugs, but as these were costly, they typically were laid down only in rooms reserved for entertaining. Inventive homeowners made do by painting small floorcloths on canvas or creating rag runners or braided rugs from recycled cloth to place beside a bed or in a hallway.

Multicultural legacy

Many cultures have made their mark on the American country style, including the Anglo-Saxons, the French, Germans, Scandinavians, Dutch and, in the Southwest and California, the Spanish. All have bequeathed an impressive legacy of furnishings and fabrics to what has evolved into a multicultural mix— the American country style.

A modern kitchen employs a vocabulary that speaks to country roots: the floor and a wooden door have natural finishes, pantry cabinets give the appearance of a freestanding cupboard and most-used utensils hang out in the open over the island.

◀ Early American beds typically exhibited a simple silhouette. Many were built high off the floor so that a smaller trundle bed could slide beneath. Beds were tied with rope that supported thin mattresses filled with horsehair. Bedding was layered, with blankets, coverlets and quilts providing warmth.

▼ American pioneer women were justifiably proud of their needlework skills, and the stitchery patterns joining the layers of their quilts often demonstrated sophisticated designs that were even more complex than the actual pattern made by quilt blocks or stripes, called *bars*.

ROBERT HARDING PICTURE LIBRARY – CHRISTOPHER DRAKE

ROBERT HARDING PICTURE LIBRARY – STEVE TANNER

◀ Many pieces of everyday furniture were painted, both as decoration and as a protective measure to prolong the life of the piece. Over time, this original paint—usually milk paint—wore away, leaving behind a patina that is now prized by collectors. Painted pieces might be further embellished with calligraphy or stencils or freehand designs.

◀ American country has been influenced by other rustic country styles. This sinuous ladder-back, rush-seated settee is just one example of what is being imported from the south of France.

Painted furniture

What the settlers' houses lacked in opulence, they made up for in warmth and color. Simulate the milk paints of old with paints in a matte finish. Work with slightly muted colors for an antique look. Accessorize your country-style rooms with baskets, wreaths, dried herbs and flowers. One perennially cheerful and stimulating color combination is red and green.

Accents of black and yellow add interest to a scheme of red, green and cream.

Natural wood

Smooth waxed or polished floors are a highlight of the American country style. Natural wood accents also abound: stacked Shaker-style oval boxes in cherry or maple, firkins, barrels, treen wares, butter churns— the list goes on and on. Set off woods with homespun fabrics. If you cannot find the antique of your dreams, charming reproductions are readily available.

Muted marine green is warmed by the glowing ruddy tone of the wood floor.

Pretty windows

Window treatments should not be complicated by hardware or fussy trimmings. One of the prettiest and most basic window treatments is a pair of cotton curtains gathered on a pole; to draw more attention to the window, cap it with a matching valance. Another option is cafe curtains; these suit tall windows and are especially charming in a kitchen or bathroom.

When using bright printed cottons, keep the overall decorating scheme simple.

Accessories

In the early American home, accessories were purely functional. Even items we consider now beyond the realm of pure utility, like the quilt, were made to be used. Everything was expected to last; virtually nothing was disposable. Many items were initially crafted in wood, but as other materials, such as cast iron and tin, became available, they began, in special cases, to replace wood. Tin was often painted to prevent rust. Special pieces, such as clocks, were handed down from generation to generation and were thus embellished for posterity.

Texture

As the American country look has evolved, it has become more textural. One way to achieve texture is to create a faux finish on walls, using techniques such as sponging or lime-washing. Work with a sponge or a rag or even crumpled plastic wrap to create the effect you want. Paint an undercoat, let it dry, then apply a top coat with your tool of choice for the final finish you desire.

Shaker style

Shaker furnishings were meticulously crafted. Spare of silhouette, they were left unadorned. Among the Shakers' more familiar inventions are the flat broom, the clothes hanger and the pegboard, from which chairs could be hung when not in use.

Woods

Because they were readily available, warm-toned woods, such as maple, cherry, cedar, pine and oak, were used for paneling and trimming out a room. First-growth trees produced wide planks; some old floors have planks as much as 18" wide. Most wood floors today are oak and are laid out in strips. For a country touch, consider stenciling a border around your floor.

Checks

Of all fabric motifs you might choose for your decorating scheme, none is more popular than the check. Some are subtle and look rather like tartans; others are big and bold. One, called the buffalo check, plays black against a rich hue such as red, green or blue.

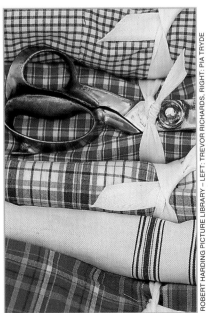

Storage

Early settlers came up with myriad ways to store household goods. Clothes and linens were stored in chests and cupboards. The Shakers were ingenious at designing banks of built-in storage with deep or shallow drawers, depending on their needs. Freestanding storage pieces are a hallmark of American country style.

Buttermilk and crimson

The color scheme of this charming bedroom was inspired by the patches of the antique quilt on the bed. The shades have been successfully translated in the curtains, and the whole effect is brightened by buttermilk yellow walls.

Harmonious, eclectic and, above all, comfortable, the traditional English country-house style is as popular today as it was in centuries past.

English Country Style

English country style, once epitomized by the grand country retreats of the landed gentry, has acquired a timeless elegance that is perfect in the modern-day home. Its appeal lies in its adaptability, for it is a look that can be achieved over a period of years, altered and added to in order to meet the changing needs of your family. As such, it should not cost a fortune and, what's more, it will never go out of style.

The style is based on an eclectic mix of furniture, fabrics and wallcoverings drawn from various sources. The only rule is that they should all blend harmoniously, creating a comforting, restful look.

Essential color

The color scheme of the country-house style is of utmost importance, for it is this that draws the elements of a room together. Shades are muted, inspired by the countryside, and usually based around a simple combination: pink and green, yellow and red, peach or apricot and white. The link with natural elements is also emphasized in the choice of materials. Cotton, linen and wool ▶

Color theory

■ The colors of the English country house should be rich and fresh but not overly bright, with creamy neutral or soft, faded white background tones. Where white walls, ceiling and woodwork are appropriate, choose a soft muted shade or off-white rather than a stark white and opt for an eggshell or a flat finish rather than a gloss finish for woodwork.

■ Colors taken from the garden combine well in the country house. Use leaf greens, with subtle rose reds and pinks; strong lilacs and paler wisteria mauves; delphinium, lobelia and viola blues; and primrose and laburnum yellows.

Garden poppy

Classic country-house shades of pink and green are used here to create a timeless look. The lead is taken from the sumptuous and comfortable brocade sofa; the walls, fabric and accessories have been carefully chosen to blend.

Yellow highlights

The bright daffodil colors of the striped wallpaper give this kitchen a light, sunny feel. The colors are echoed in the trim of the floral curtain, whose peach-and-blue print coordinates well with the rug on the tiled floor.

■ Clear sky blues with sunny yellows and golds add warmth and an impression of space to small kitchens and dining rooms. The more exotic Regency colors— faded lacquer or Indian red combined with warm golds and cream—can have sharp touches of jade or delft blue. Add brass accessories for a more formal scheme.

Country-house bathrooms were simple affairs; functional, rather than beautiful. Here, the simple philosophy has been transformed with the clever addition of decorative objects—all featuring shells. The intricacy of such accessories is shown to good effect against the plain cream backdrop of the woodwork.

◀ **This dining room has been put together with a variety of furniture in different styles and woods. The simplicity of the furniture's design coupled with the use of muted browns and cream on walls and fabric create a cohesive whole.**

fabrics are ideal for curtains, shades, bedding and upholstery—with opulent silk for best. One type of fabric long associated with English country style is chintz—a pretty (often glazed) cotton with a floral design. The word *chintz* is derived from the Hindu *chint,* a painted Indian calico cloth.

Furniture

Cozy comfort best describes the style of upholstered furniture, which is designed in simple shapes to support the back, head and neck—and with enough depth for the longest legs. Sofas and deep chairs often have side wings, originally designed to keep out drafts.

Related fabric designs for upholstery provide a decorative link—chairs and sofas of different shapes used together are more interesting than the conventional three-piece suite. For example, a bold floral design centered on a large sofa can be combined with plain and striped chair slipcovers and a companion check or a plaid on a smaller sofa.

In a small living room, a padded window seat built into a bay window can provide a space-saving solution. Covered to coordinate with the rest of the furnishings, it draws attention to the window and the view beyond.

Window treatments should never be too opulent—prettily patterned or floral

lightweight materials work best. The fabric can be carried through to cushions or needlepoint pillows, and throws can be used to integrate items into the theme. Table covers can also help draw elements together.

Mixing and matching

The clever mixing of different styles of furniture is an essential feature of the English country look—a variety of disparate items can be drawn together by color-washing or with a stenciled pattern. Or different woods can be combined, such as the warm golden tones of pine and satinwood with the reddish tones of cherry and mahogany.

► This pretty bedroom has a delicate floral theme, with the accents on soft pink and peach. Pale apricot walls provide a harmonious backdrop, with dark and light woods combined to good effect.

▼ The focus of this inviting living room is the floral pattern on the embroidered pillows. The muted tones are carried through to the lampshade and even to the pretty floral arrangements on the tables and in the wall sconce. The wall color provides a mellow backdrop, and the soft pink shade is echoed in the throw.

◄ Warm butter yellow on walls and fabric work together with the honey tones of old wood in this airy dining room. Carved wooden dining chairs provide an effective contrast to the stripped pine table and floor, and lush, leafy green plants, trailing over the mantelpiece and filling the ornamental crib, soften the starkness of the room.

► Shades of green provide the color in this spacious country-house bedroom. Pale mint green on the walls coupled with apple white on the woodwork give the room a fresh, summery feel. The brass bed stands alongside classic period furnishings of a Lloyd loom chair and light scrubbed pine.

Summer fields

Shades of ripe corn with splashes of scarlet poppy, buttercup yellow with wine-rich burgundy—the colors of late summer fields are the perfect solution for a country-style home. The look is never pristine, so antique fabrics and faded colors work just as well as crisp new materials. Choose simply styled curtains in large easy prints and go for old-fashioned patterns on slipcovers and throws.

Reds, yellows and burgundies are perfect for bedrooms and living rooms.

Orchard blossom

The combination of pale pink and green is one of the most appealing of all color schemes in the country-house interior. Inspired by hedgerows of wild roses, apple blossom orchards and wildflower meadows, the colors should be soft and similar in tone. All kinds of wood work well with these shades, from light stripped pine to deep polished mahogany, and this gives a wide scope for furnishings.

Shades of pink and green give a fresh feel to living rooms.

Spring flowers

Bright yellow, rich terra-cotta, deep blue and green bring the glow of spring sunshine to any room. Warm colors used over large areas, such as walls and floors, make an ideal backdrop for richly patterned rugs and floral fabrics and work well with light, natural woods. Opt for an eggshell or a flat finish on painted surfaces to maintain the soft matte effect throughout and stick to shades of color rather than stark white.

Bright yellows, reds and greens blend with rich browns and blues to brighten up any kitchen.

Timeless accessories

The eclectic style of the country home leaves plenty of options when it comes to accessories. Family heirlooms combine with junk-shop finds to complete a rich collection of artifacts. Opt for traditional rather than contemporary—real candle sconces, homemade potpourri and grasses picked from the garden and dried give an authentic country feel.

ROBERT HARDING PICTURE LIBRARY

BOTH PICTURES: ROBERT HARDING PICTURE LIBRARY

Country-house chintz

Pretty, delicate accessories are ideal for the traditional country chintz look. Crisp white china with a floral design in shades of pink and green echoes the look of spring flowers. Side tables, mantels and shelves can be arranged with ornaments and curios set out to form a harmonious display. Boxes, lamps, candleholders and novelty objects, such as birdcages, placed on a pretty tablecloth make attractive accents. Small picture frames in silver, gold and porcelain used to display miniature portraits or family photographs are also popular and traditional accessories.

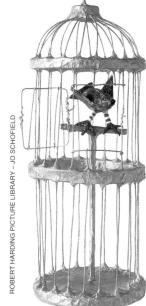

ROBERT HARDING PICTURE LIBRARY – JO SCHOFIELD

ROBERT HARDING PICTURELIBRARY

ROBERT HARDING PICTURE LIBRARY – BILL BATTEN

A china tea set elegantly styled with a classic motif can set the tone for the room.

The rustic look

Bringing the outside in is a policy that did not stop with plants in the country house interior. All aspects of nature were embraced, particularly in the kitchen. In today's adaptation of the style, copper molds in the forms of rabbits and fish, duck decoys and framed animal prints add liveliness to a room. These can be coupled with the decorative accoutrements of outdoor pursuits, such as fishing rods, vintage wooden tennis rackets and wicker picnic baskets.

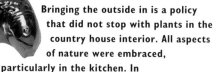

ALL PICTURES: ROBERT HARDING PICTURE LIBRARY

13

Mediterranean

Whether you love its rustic textures or its brilliant colors, the Mediterranean is an exciting source of inspiration that can give any room in your home a touch of warmth and flavor.

Sun-baked shades

Take your natural inspiration from the warmth of the colors found around the Mediterranean. Even the neutral shades here take on a sunny quality—and, in the room pictured above, they mix well with the warmth of the wood and the rich textures of the soft furnishings.

These are the colors that make you feel as though you've let the sunshine into your home. The distinctive warm, earthy colors—deep terra-cottas, rich ochers, sunny golds, glowing pinks, subtle wine reds and natural stones, café au lait and warm beiges—are often used as a sharp contrast with cooler colors—clear blues, strong greens and vivid turquoise—which all help to emphasize the warmth of the overall effect. They are often seen in areas like Provence, where the exterior walls of cottages are color-washed in rich, earthy tones; the shutters and woodwork are sharply contrasted in blues or greens, which take on a rubbed patina when bleached by the sun.

Natural warmth

This style is very much influenced by the Mediterranean countryside—and the climate. Local terra-cotta, wood and other natural products are ▶

STYLE

Bold strokes

All these warm touches can be added quickly and cheaply with accessories, such as pottery, earthenware, pillows, rugs or table covers; a chair or two; a piece of painted furniture; or a colorful wall treatment, making the Mediterranean style a fairly easy one to copy on the smallest of budgets.

A fresh look

If you want to introduce an alfresco atmosphere to a room, try painting the walls—and even the ceiling—a vivid sky blue. Lots of sparkling white touches will add to that fresh-air feeling.

Color theory

■ Hot and warm colors always need some cool contrast to offset them, creating a complementary, or contrasting, color scheme. The warm, advancing color will always appear to dominate, so if you want a scheme to look equally proportioned, use about one-third of the warm tone to two-thirds of the cool one for maximum effect.

■ If you are going to create a bold complementary scheme, remember to relate the strength of the color to the size of the space where it is being featured. Bold colors can be used for the main surfaces (on walls, for window treatments, on a floor or on an "important" piece of furniture) when you have a large space or kept to interesting accents (rugs and throws, pottery, table settings, pillows) and smaller items (painted wooden chairs or small cabinets) when the room size is more modest.

■ Quality of light is important too. Natural daylight will show the true colors, but at night you may need background lighting to bathe the room in a warm glow; then you can provide strategic accent or display lighting to focus on important features or colors.

▼ Simple, rustic styles make the most of wooden textures. Add accessories that use natural fibers, such as wicker and raffia woven into baskets to display dried herbs and flowers, together with lots of chunky, glazed pottery.

ROBERT HARDING PICTURE LIBRARY – BROCK

▲ Terra-cotta pots make ideal kitchenware. In natural shades or glazed in bright blues, greens and ochers to complement colored kitchen tiles, they offset foods beautifully. And clay flowerpots are perfect for showing off a prized collection of herbs, brightly colored geraniums or ivy topiaries.

all much used here. Textures are just as robust as the colors. Rough-hewn or distressed wood is used for furniture—including cupboards and cabinets with chicken-wire doors, rather than more formal glass-fronted pieces. Rush seats on benches and chairs, simple wooden seats softened with tie-on cushions, scrubbed wooden or tile-topped dining tables and the "crumbly" distorted quality of a piece of driftwood used as an objet d'art, are all integral to this style.

Rich harvests

Because the culinary arts are so important in this part of the world, Mediterranean style is just the look to adapt for a kitchen or dining room. With so much natural produce on hand—from olives and peppers to eggplant, tomatoes and fruits— you will find all the rich colors a useful source for your decorating ideas. Many meals are taken alfresco on sun-baked balconies and patios— screened with vines or other lush climbing plants trained on trellises or pergolas overhead. This type of outdoor theme is ideal for a dining room,

and wall stencils showing bunches of purple grapes and glossy green leaves would look good with houseplants next to a wall. Other suitable motifs include trailing nasturtiums in vivid gold, flame red and burnt orange with yellow-green leaves; bright pink, purple and red bougainvilleas; feathery fronds of yellow mimosa with gray-green foliage. It is a style that works equally well in a small apartment, a modest ranch house or a large country house.

Seashore influences

Seashore motifs find a natural home in the Mediterranean-style bathroom. You can use seashells, pebbles and pieces of driftwood as accessories and you can easily echo starfish, shell or crustacean shapes with a stenciled pattern on the walls or even on the top of a wooden toilet seat! Use sun, sand and sea-bleached neutral shades offset against natural wood with a similar, faded look. Introduce more color with brilliant sky blue touches, such as fleecy towels, and rich terra-cotta accents, such as flowerpots.

◀ Walls are often left plain or color-washed, which helps to create a textured effect. In this example, the style relies on striking colors in the decor and on the patterns in the soft furnishings for its impact.

▶ Interesting textures also apply to the building structure itself—whether as exposed stone walls (pictured right) or as roughly plastered walls or as basic paneling on lower wall areas, which are then limed or color-washed. Ceiling beams, distressed or limed, can be a feature too.

Ceramic, clay or stone tiles are often the original flooring or else they are salvaged from an old farmhouse. Soften the effect with rush matting or textured rugs and add warmth with brightly colored pillows or slipcovers.

▲ Furniture is very basic in the Mediterranean bedroom. Beds are wood-framed with carved headboards and footboards or boat-shaped, or else they are made of metal, matte painted (never shiny) in white, black or a rich, deep color. Other items may include a wooden freestanding cupboard, a bedside table and a linen chest.

Warm neutrals

Whether you use them alone or mixed with touches of mellowed brighter colors, choose neutral shades that have a warm slant. Pick soft beiges, creams, pinky mushroom and milky coffee colors. Avoid the cold gray neutrals, which will make warm colors look out of place in a room with a northern exposure.

Neutral shades that have taken on a warm tone always look more welcoming.

Mellowed brights

To achieve an authentic look, these colors need to be rich and deep but not as strong as primary colors. Look for terra-cottas and saffron rather than a "hot" pure orange; Provençal pinks and wine reds instead of scarlet; denim, sky or Mediterranean blue or even turquoise rather than royal blue; jade, gray-green or lime in place of grass green; plus sunshine golds and deep ocher yellows.

The beauty of these rich colors is that they give even a small space more impact.

Rustic harmony

You can put either of these color schemes to work with the rustic touches that create a true harmony of Mediterranean style. And if you don't have roughly plastered walls or ceilings with exposed beams, try laying tile or wood flooring, choose simple furnishings and decor, and soften the effect with a handful of handcrafted items—woven rugs, pottery and pillows in country-style prints.

The shades of bleached and faded rustic textures create a relaxing, lived-in atmosphere.

Practical ideas

Accessories are not there for looks alone—they are a useful and an integral part of the style, arranged for maximum efficiency as well as visual impact. In the kitchen, pots, pans, whisks and other cooking utensils may be suspended from a rail or chain—close at hand and decorative at the same time. Earthenware, china and colorful pottery and casseroles plus decorative glassware may be displayed on open shelves; and the scrubbed kitchen table, used for food preparation, may be covered with a Provençal tablecloth when it comes to family mealtimes.

Colors that inspire

Mediterranean colors are associated with painters such as Monet (his famous yellow dining room) and Van Gogh (sunflowers, cornflowers, poppies, and his lavender blues and herb greens). They were also made popular in the 1920s and '30s by the costumes and stage sets for Diaghilev's Ballet Russe de Monte Carlo. You'll find the rich colors are combined in textiles too—especially Provençal cottons and linen weaves—as well as on ceramic tiles and in faience ware and china.

Room to relax in

The Mediterranean bedroom may be basic—but it has an intrinsic style. Quilted bedcovers are made in simple cotton, perhaps with a Provençal design or in a characteristic woven check. Bed linen is either pure linen or cotton, with a little self-colored trimming or embroidery. Window treatments are simple—unadorned shutters may be used or else cane or traditional roller shades, the latter trimmed with lace or crochet, a type of trimming that is also popular for edging a display shelf.

Color theory

■ Aim for a good tonal balance with these color schemes—even if you are going for a contrast. Combine ocher with turquoise, strong peach with emerald green, terra-cotta with mint green, apricot with jade tones, wine red with laurel green and, for the brighter shades, chrome yellow or sunflower gold with sky blue.

Color theory

■ To create a truly Mediterranean flavor, you will want the warmth of your color scheme to be predominant, so use half warm to half cool shades, or for a really cozy effect, use two-thirds warm colors to one-third cool colors.

Color theory

■ If you would prefer to enhance the warm atmosphere, you can use mainly sunny colors—with warm neutrals—and introduce some sharp, cool colors in your accents and accessories to emphasize the warm colors.

ETHNIC style

Influences from far-flung lands **add their own** special richness and texture **to fashions in interior design.**

Natural wood

Sand-colored walls and wooden carvings, bowls and furniture create a dining room with an African flavor. Louvered doors and shutters filter the light.

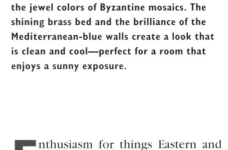

Moorish style

The dazzling patterns of this bedspread echo the jewel colors of Byzantine mosaics. The shining brass bed and the brilliance of the Mediterranean-blue walls create a look that is clean and cool—perfect for a room that enjoys a sunny exposure.

A modern interpretation

A stony-neutral scheme with darkly contrasting accessories echoes a traditional Middle Eastern look. The low glass table, geometric patterned rug and intricately carved woodwork emphasize the ethnic theme.

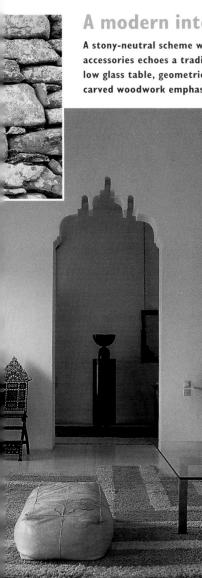

Enthusiasm for things Eastern and exotic began in earnest after trade routes to the East were opened and ships brought goods and decorative accessories from China—initially via the English trade and then directly to America. Those Oriental tastes and fashions adopted by the monied classes were soon copied by the less-affluent country folk.

During the 18th century, worldwide trade flourished, and attention turned to the outside world. Artifacts unearthed at Greek excavations rekindled interest in the ancient heritage of Greece and Rome and focused attention on styles based on classical antiquity. Expeditions to Egypt at the turn of the 19th century spurred interest in Egyptian design and motifs, both in furniture and as an overall design theme.

New influences

The 1876 Centennial Exposition in Philadelphia, which featured examples of goods and artifacts from all over the world, brought the fad for Japanese-style accessories and furniture and sparked interest in Turkish-style designs and Moorish arched windows. Architects, builders, decorators and manufacturers worked these Oriental, Indian and African themes and motifs into their buildings, products and interiors, and those influences are apparent in the styles of the day.

Less than 100 years later, there ▶

Color theory

■ Hand-decorated Chinese wallpaper panels once were the most fashionable, exotic and expensive wall treatments available. These were often framed with fretwork trim with an oriental-style motif. Lacquered cabinets in red, black and gold were used to display foreign treasures. A lot of furniture was designed with an oriental look, and Thomas Chippendale adapted the style to create his famous Chinese Chippendale pieces.

■ The Raj-style scheme looks good based on soft natural or neutral colors—subtle browns, creams and beiges and the natural colors of wood. Creamy muslins, unbleached cottons, linens and calicos add a pale, soft touch. Animal prints incorporate extra visual interest, and a few touches of vivid color—terra-cotta, golden yellow, peacock blue or deep green— add color contrast.

■ For a more modern Oriental theme, use low-slung furniture— futons, short carved wooden coffee tables, floor cushions—simple sliding screens or pierced panels with oriental motifs, and minimal window treatments. Add one eye-catching ceramic pot filled with twisted twigs or one exotic bloom to give a softer edge to the lines of the room.

◄ This New Mexico living room has an adobe fireplace with American Indian pottery and Navajo wall hangings and rugs. If you are lucky enough to have a big fireplace such as this, make the most of it with some well-chosen accessories and plenty of foliage for contrasting color accents.

▼ Without echoing any particular national style, this landing has a distinctly foreign atmosphere, created by the rattan blind, patterned rug, shiny natural wood floor, plain stone walls and natural pottery—a little piece of the exotic East in the city.

▼ The various elements of this Bahrain interior—gold-embroidered cushions in dazzling reds, greens and maroon, colored glassware, ornate mirrors—create an exotic style, and traditional carpets contribute to the atmosphere.

◀ This Moorish-style bedroom and bath are divided by elegant, light-filtering open-worked screen doors, with gold embroidered throws and ornate wall hangings adding to the authentic Middle Eastern feel.

▶ Contrast in form is important—square cushions and wall hangings provide a foil for the carved screen, inlaid tables and brass lamp in a room that strikes a happy balance between contemporary and Moroccan.

was a revival of interest in all things ethnic, especially the African influence, which brought bright earthy colors and animal prints into the decorating scene and re-introduced the use of unusual and exotic houseplants and African art.

Acquiring the style

Ethnic styles, being by nature eclectic, allow you to adapt themes and collect items from a variety of sources; you just need a deft touch to put them together effectively.

Today there is a great deal of imported cane and bamboo furniture, and fabrics, accessories and lighting with an ethnic "feel" available—and most items are very reasonably priced. But you do not have to spend a fortune, nor slavishly buy everything from just one country—in fact, many of the most attractive schemes are built up over time as you discover just the right piece of furniture or accessory at a flea market or at auction—or bring it back from a trip abroad. The huge variety of furniture and accessories in stores should make it easy to achieve just the ethnic style you want.

▲ Combine wood, soft natural leather, unglazed pottery, ethnic woven rugs and a background of whitewashed plastered walls for a warm, fresh and spacious look reminiscent of Mexican ranch house style.

Wood tones

Broken sunlight filtering into a room full of warm, natural wood creates a comfortable, easy-to-live-with atmosphere. There is no need to be slavish about the authenticity of accessories, such as crockery or tableware—anything made with natural, untreated materials will contribute to the overall ethnic feel of a room such as this.

Warm naturals—woody browns, sandy yellows and fruity greens are comfortable to live with.

Jewel colors

Although the bed is an ornate piece of furniture, the focal point of this bedroom is the brilliantly colored bedspread with its patchwork of traditional Middle Eastern designs. You don't need to travel far to find fabric or bed linen like this—import shops are increasingly common all around the country, stocking exotic items, large and small, at modest prices.

Brilliant colors echo the traditional mosaics of Middle Eastern lands.

Cool sophistication

Everything in this room is designed to increase the feeling of cool space and airiness. The high ceiling, pale neutral color scheme and elegant furniture create a peaceful atmosphere. However, the room is quite stark. The edges can be softened by window shades, curtains or drapes in a light-filtering fabric, such as muslin or very fine cotton, and by plants or foliage in various colors and shapes.

Monochromatic and neutral colors tend to make any room appear airier.

Basic elements

This type of wood-toned ethnic theme needs plenty of textural and color contrast—dark shiny metal, as in the candlesticks on the left, nubby fabrics, such as the rag rugs below left, and glowing natural wood. Robust wooden pieces, such as the carved leaf and bird bowls, add just the right flavor, as do big, chunky pieces of pottery. The more natural materials you use, the more effective this sort of theme will look—seek out carved accessories or functional items from markets and import shops so that you gradually collect all the elements that give the room its own special ethnic feel.

Color theory

■ Use unbleached canvas, hung on a simple wooden pole at cornice height, as a covering for walls or as a screen for windows. This would work well in a wood-toned, neutral color scheme with folding canvas campaign-style chairs. If you want the look of wall-to-wall carpeting, use a beige Berber carpet as a base for patterned rugs.

Exotic and opulent

For an Arabian Nights look, nothing can beat the opulence of a tented ceiling as on the right, with soft drapes and wall hangings around it. You can translate this traditional look with some of the fabulous colors and soft textures of modern fabrics. Use several shades of the same color with different designs for maximum effect. Brass Moorish accessories, such as the hanging lamp, are perfect, as are the two gold frames on the left.

If traditional brass or carved wood furniture are hard to find or too ornate for your taste, you might consider a more modern version—an upholstered iron-framed chair, as on the right.

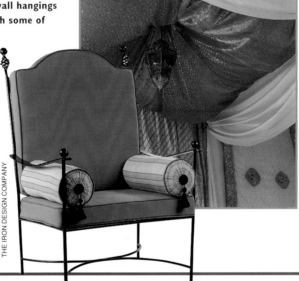

Color theory

■ Adapt a Middle Eastern look for a more contemporary room. There are many Kilim patterns reproduced on fabrics and upholstery that would make a perfect starting point for the scheme. Use those patterns for rugs or wall hangings, or for a selection of floor cushions to create a floor-level sitting area.

Ethnic artifacts

Against a light background, dark accessories and furniture have a strong visual impact—and if they are large enough to stand alone on the floor or on a pedestal (bottom left), they can be particularly striking. For added dramatic effect, use candlelight to supplement table lamps or side lights—sconces are in fashion and are available to suit any sort of setting, plain or elaborate. If you want to add color to a pale neutral scheme, add some rugs with geometric patterns and in richly dyed woven materials—the Indian-style rugs (above left) will fit comfortably into this style of room.

Color theory

■ Part of the secret of success is to work with one theme, either provided by color; by specific patterns; by pieces of furniture, fabrics, soft furnishings and window treatments; or by a special collection of accessories cleverly displayed. Highlight important pieces with display or accent lighting.

25

Kitchens

The kitchen used to be one of the forgotten corners of the home as far as decorating was concerned. Today it is recognized as the hub of the household, with an importance and style all its own.

Rustic warmth

This nostalgic country-style kitchen is a functional and friendly family gathering place. The open cupboard, wooden beams, hanging pots, baskets and dried flowers reflect nature's warmth in the comfortable colors and textures of the woodlands.

Today the kitchen is often an extension of the family room—a place for informal entertaining—so it has again become the true heart of the home, as it was centuries ago. But unlike in those days, there is now a wonderful selection of decorating styles, colors and designs to choose from.

Color schemes

There is no reason kitchen colors should not create just the mood you want—or suggest a specific period style or design theme, such as Shaker, Scandinavian, Mediterranean or metropolitan.

Most important, the style should echo the overall architectural character of your house and suit the function of the area, so select suitable surface treatments, paying particular attention to safety, ease of cleaning and practicality.

Kitchens are often hot rooms, but can also be cold and clinical, so choose a scheme to suit your house. Pale lavender will look warm with maize gold and soft cream. Or for a really sunny effect, use warm ocher with sky blue, teamed with white and touches of rich green. Or combine herb greens with corn golds and paler sorbet yellows.

Textural contrast is a vital aspect of good design. Soften the often hard lines of a ▶

Elegant neutrals

A neutral scheme that tends toward a creamy pale pink color is ideal for a spacious kitchen, where books, bottles, spices and accessories can be displayed at their best without making the kitchen look cluttered. Curtains and upholstery in a dining area should be easy to clean or launder.

Economical and bright

Remember that red is an appetite-inducing color—but that it can also make meat look undercooked if used near the oven. The shiny tomato red (left) is offset by strong green accents and textural contrast in the sisal carpet.

Color theory

■ Consider the direction the kitchen faces, the amount of natural daylight it receives (and the evening lighting), its size and shape, the existing climate and the mood you want to create. A kitchen may be hot, especially in a warm climate, so a scheme based on cool colors can be very effective. Try subtle sage green with blue-lilac and touches of sharp lime contrasted with white or a scheme based on blues, warmed up with touches of terra-cotta and cream. A neutral mix of black, white, silver and gray brightened with some tomato red or sunflower yellow accents can be very effective.

■ In a cold kitchen, pink can be very unusual and comforting. Combine sugar pink with deep crushed raspberry and a little dove gray; navy blue or purple accents would add a sophisticated touch. Lemon with burnt orange, peach and chestnut brown softened with cream will look rich and inviting. Warmer neutrals based on wood tones will be relaxing but may need strong contrasting accents to avoid looking bland. For a more subtle effect, try sugary pastels—pink, lemon, lime, lilac or apricot can look really appetizing in a kitchen.

▲ aShiny chrome or stainless steel brighten the look of a more contemporary kitchen, giving highlights to even the most monochromatic of schemes. If this is not possible, add light with a low-luster enamel finish on the walls and a gloss finish for the woodwork, baseboards, and window and door frames.

▲ Decorative containers can enhance shelves and wall-mounted cabinets, adding character and interest—these hand-painted jars and original tiles make a unique feature of an old-fashioned cabinet.

kitchen with tablecloths, chair cushions and decorative lace or other fabric shelf trims. For a permanent decorative shelf edging, you can also get a soft effect with trellis or perforated hardboard painted to contrast with the shelf.

Tile potential

In addition to using colored grout to brighten up old tile, you can tile directly over existing tile, as long as you use the proper mastic to firmly attach the new tile. Use tiles that have little projections on the edges and are self-spacing.

Install the tiles in a more original way than squarely—perhaps in diamond shapes or with a patterned tile here and there. Or use border tiles to define a panel or tiled backsplash, then echo the motif with a stencil along the bottom edge of your table linen or roller shades.

Kitchen cabinets

If you cannot afford to replace your existing cabinets, sand, prime and paint them, then use any of a multitude of paint

To give kitchen cabinets a face-lift, buy standard cabinet doors and drawer fronts from home improvement stores. Be sure the hinges and frames are strong enough to hold the new fronts. Or buy self-adhesive panels to stick to existing doors and drawers for a new look.

◄ If you have poorly plastered walls, enhance the effect with an impasto finish and color-wash over the top for a cottagey look. Or if you want to cover an existing wall finish, use tongue-and-groove paneling; wood-wash or stain the paneling and seal it with a matte or semi-matte varnish.

▼ Modern cabinetry meets the original country kitchen (below). Clever use of decorative tiles softens the look of the custom cabinets to blend with the cupboard and new brick-and-wood island with built-in stove. With good planning and a main look in mind, you can make all sorts of features fit together.

▲ Kitchens often have cold shiny surfaces—ceramic tiles, gloss paint, laminates and metal. Soften and diffuse these by filtering light through slatted blinds and adding plants for color and texture.

effects, such as graining, dragging or stenciling, to decorate them. This is also a good way of integrating a new cabinet into an existing scheme.

Give work surfaces a fresh look with attractive countertop tiles or install a new laminated countertop. Other options include scrubbable hardwood, granite or even marble, but remember that the latter are very heavy, so check the strength of the frames before you order new countertops.

Safety first

When planning your kitchen, think safety! Choose nonslip flooring; easy-clean, hygienic work surfaces; and practical directional lighting. Be sure to hang light fixtures high enough so that you can't bump into them. Avoid using fussy window treatments, which can be a fire hazard if hung too near the range. If you bear all this in mind, your kitchen will be a safe place in which to cook, eat and socialize.

Warm and woodsy

Hang attractive pots and pans on hooks positioned close to your work surfaces and stove for practical use. Even if you base a rustic look around mainly modern pieces of wooden furniture, some well-chosen, authentic traditional items, such as the old church pews and a well-worn table, will help establish a comfortable farmhouse atmosphere.

Natural colors and untreated wood create a relaxing countrified feel.

Cool and airy

Textures, such as the grille over the radiator at the window, the detailing over the range hood and the cane of the chairs give visual interest in an essentially plain room. Both overhead lighting in the dining area and task lighting, which can be directed over work areas or attached underneath wall cabinets to illuminate countertops, are important.

Soft pastels and unpatterned surfaces increase the impression of space.

Rustic harmony

Existing tiles are not impossible to decorate. You can transform ceramic tiles by painting them, as long as they are properly primered. Or for an even cheaper transformation, regrout tiles with colored grout. You can buy ready-made grout in a fairly restricted color range, but if you cannot find the shade you want, add poster paint or powder pigment to plain white grout to create your own.

Primary red with sandy yellow and accents in green create a stimulating atmosphere.

ROBERT HARDING PICTURE LIBRARY – BRIAN HARRISON

Traditional cottage style

Bunches of dried flowers and herbs in terra-cotta pots will not make a kitchen workable, but they help to create ambience. The kitchen is a room where necessary items, such as storage containers of pasta, bottles filled with herb vinegars and special oils, can make an attractive display. Select traditional furniture, such as a rocking chair or a grandfather clock, along with pottery, cookware and dinnerware in a rustic, cottagey style to add to the overall look of the room.

ROBERT HARDING PICTURE LIBRARY

Style for a kitchen-dining area

Use accessories to add accent colors—to warm up a cool scheme, cool down a hot one or add spice to a neutral or monochromatic scheme. Usually, fussy, ornate accessories do not work well in a kitchen, but if you have a large kitchen that includes a dining area, add some pretty accessories in the form of china or table linen that fit in with the main style and look of the functional part of the kitchen. Practical accessories, such as cookie molds, and decorative pieces like this gilded wall wreath add to the ambience of a kitchen and give it that special comfortable, lived-in and welcoming look.

PHOTO – LUCINDA SYMONS

Smart and shiny

A modern kitchen, planned on a careful budget, can look coordinated and classy with the right accessories and basic kitchen equipment. Simple, inexpensive, brightly colored kitchenware and utensils not only serve a culinary function but add to the decor too. Quite different from the cool and expensive elegance of chrome, steel and smoked glass seen in many designer kitchens, bold brass, shiny scales and colorful canisters work with other accessories to create a matching, chic look—on a budget!

PHOTO – J TUSBY

COUNTRY

Country kitchen

Wood floors and cabinets, wicker furniture and terra-cotta crocks contribute to a country look in a big eat-in kitchen. The walls, painted a soft duck-egg blue, show only a hint of color. The country feel comes from the use of predominantly natural materials.

The rustic look is one of today's most popular styles—a way for city dwellers to enjoy a touch of the country. Discover how to achieve the look using color and natural materials and fabrics.

Color is the single most important factor in a decorating scheme—your first ally when you want to transform your home. Although there is a huge color palette from which to choose, by far the most popular and easiest colors to work with are the neutrals, which create a relaxed and quiet atmosphere without being boring. The only true neutrals are black, white and gray, but so-called natural neutrals have a definite character of their own. However, some natural whites can relate back to the original hues and can be disappointing in use, looking like wishy-washy shadows of their original colors.

Back to nature

Many of the most effective neutrals are undyed natural products, each with its own color and texture. Those include materials such as crunchy coir, sisal, rush and sea grass matting for floor coverings and unbleached cotton and calico, creamy canvas, raw silk, off-white muslin, lace and voile for window treatments and bedcovers.

Rustic greens

Green is an ideal color for a natural look—the color of foliage, as above, and grass, moss and fields. The plaster walls in this room have been painted a light green for a gentle rustic feel; time has softened and aged the plaster and mellowed the wood of the bench to create a relaxed and peaceful country feel. Accessories, such as painted plates and wildflowers, extend the look.

ROBERT HARDING PICTURE LIBRARY; INSET, THE IMAGE BANK

naturals

Red browns

A room does not need to be rustic and naive in its style to benefit from the warm and relaxing atmosphere created by country colors. These harvest shades—warm colors of beans, lentils and rice—and the natural textures of fiber floor coverings can look sophisticated and modern to suit an apartment in the city as well as a country cottage.

Color theory

■ Avoid using pure white on walls in all but the smallest of rooms. Although white walls reflect light, they can also be stark, harsh and dazzling if the room receives a lot of natural light. It is better to reserve white for cornices, moldings, woodwork and trim.

■ If you are using a patterned fabric or wallcovering with a pale background, match your ceiling and woodwork color to this. Rarely is the fabric or paper base on which the pattern is printed a pure white, so use a muted cream, off-white or pinkish magnolia.

■ All the basic color-scheme principles apply when working with neutrals—the size and shape of the room and the way it faces must be taken into account. Neutral schemes tend to give a sense of space so are ideal in small rooms but can also be used to enhance a room's good features and disguise bad ones.

■ When you shop for the smaller elements of a color scheme, bring samples of any existing items with you to get a good color match. Include any built-in furniture, wood and other materials. If you have fabric swatches, check that the real thing has not changed in tone from the original sample.

33

For accessories and furniture, use wicker, rattan, cane and bamboo, and for upholstery, use wool, tweed or flax-colored linen. Complete the picture with glowing copper and brass, gleaming silver or more subtle pewter in accents such as light fixtures and accessories.

Wall treatments

You can leave walls natural to show original wood paneling or the rich colors of brick, slate or stone. Even untreated plaster can be very effective in, say, a converted barn, warehouse or cottage—but avoid using this type of surface on a property where it would be totally out of place. A neutral color scheme or a natural material, such as wool, cotton, grasscloth or silk wall covering—even eggshell paint—can create a country look without fighting the building's original style.

Give the same consideration to the use of laces and other sheer fabrics at windows and as bedding—crisp white will look right in some circumstances, especially if you decide to build up a white-on-white scheme, but in other cases, where the neutral has to relate to other surfaces, try ivory and parchment tones.

Contrasting textures

Many of these natural materials have their own distinct texture—rough, shiny, nubby, crunchy, coarsely woven, velvety or smooth. But natural/neutral schemes, more than any others, need plenty of contrast in texture to add interest and variety, especially if there is not much color or variation in tone in the scheme.

Combine the rough texture of exposed brick and stone with a soft, sheer, light-filtering fabric—then add a sharp touch of shiny metal or ceramic. Filter the light through slatted blinds, pick an eggshell or a flat finish for painted walls and woodwork, and add a few rattan items to create schemes that are countrified but modern.

If your taste is more traditional, mix mellow woods with brass, supple leather, cane, wicker and basketry, and soften the effect with lace or linens trimmed with embroidery. Complement these with earthy terra-cotta floor tile or flat stone, matte-painted wood paneling, velvety or tapestry-like woven textiles and touches of heavy iron or verdigrised metalwork.

Working with neutrals

In a neutral one-color scheme, take care to match colors accurately. In a color scheme based on creams, buttermilks and golden-browns, the overall tone is likely to be yellowish and warm, while the overall tone of a scheme based on beiges and deeper browns often relates more closely to red. If you use cooler off-whites, the effect will be cooler and closer to the blue-green end of the spectrum.

◄ **Wood is a key element in natural color schemes. You can leave it natural and simply wax or seal it as in the stairs, left, or add color with stain or paint. However, wood is usually more effective if you allow the natural grain of the wood to show through.**

◄ Rustic colors, such as warm ocher, used to color-wash the walls of this farmhouse breakfast room, are particularly effective in traditional country settings. The color complements original features, such as the ceiling beams, the natural wood of the door and the carved border above it.

▲ Natural floors, such as these heavy flagstones, usually form an integral part of the building and lend character and atmosphere to any room. Furnish a traditional country room, such as this kitchen, with its inherent style in mind, using wood and natural fibers, and accessorize with old-fashioned crockery.

◄ The texture of painted white wicker and the lacy patterns of the crocheted bedspread create a fresh, gently rustic feel. This is enhanced by the greenery of the plants and the sprigged flowers painted on the mirror.

▶ Soft creams, ivories, faded and distressed painted surfaces, and an untreated wood floor lend unsophisticated charm to an attic bed-room. All the colors are muted and easy on the eye. When choosing sheer fabrics to blend with a soft color scheme such as this, try dipping lace or net fabric in a weak solution of cold tea to prevent the white from appearing too stark.

Color theory

■ Think about the amount of light a room receives—and the type of light and at what time of day. East-facing rooms will be warm and sunny first thing in the morning but cold and dark for most of the afternoon and evening, so will benefit from pale yet warm neutral colors. These also work well in north-facing, sunless and dark rooms, which can look rather cold and unwelcoming. West- and south-facing rooms receive afternoon and evening light and tend to be warm, so they can be decorated in the cooler neutrals—the grays, combined with black and white. Pure white can be dazzling in a room with very clear north light, so use it with care.

■ You can use natural and neutral accents and accessories to tone down or to add lightness and a feeling of calm to a scheme that is based on stronger colors. The creamy-beige neutrals work well with dark reds, blues, greens and terra-cottas. Off-whites will add a sophisticated touch to midtoned rooms; the paler grays, black and white will tone down bright, jazzy schemes.

■ Get samples of materials and look at them in the actual room and under its own lighting conditions before making a final choice.

Country kitchen

Although the feel of this kitchen is distinctly country, it is bright and modern. Accessories make all the difference. If this kitchen had small-print curtains or table linen and more traditional china, it might look old-fashioned. Instead, bright, primary-colored china, such as the pitcher and mugs on the right, and fresh floral curtains create an up-to-date feel.

Flowers enhance a rustic room—select them to brighten up or subdue a scheme.

ABODE UK

CAMERA PRESS LTD, TREVOR RICHARDS

PHOTOGRAPHY BY SEAN ELLIS

Red browns

Achieving a successful tonal balance is important in neutral schemes such as this, especially if there is a lack of pattern interest. If the neutral colors are too pale, the result will be weak and bland; if everything is midtone, the room will simply look dull. To get a warm and interesting effect, use accents in dark shades and accessorize with patterns and midtones.

Natural fibers make a warm-looking and durable textured floor covering.

WICKES BUILDING SUPPLIES LTD

THRESHOLD FLOORINGS

Rustic greens

A country look with a lot of wood in furniture and flooring needs contrasts in color and texture in the form of soft furnishings—pillows, rugs or upholstery—to make it welcoming and comfortable. Here an embroidered throw adds rich color and texture and a dramatic peasant touch to a color scheme that is mainly soft green and pale blue.

Terra-cotta pots with an ethnic design add color and warmth to a country-style room.

ROBERT HARDING PICTURE LIBRARY

THE IMAGE BANK

CHAPTER 2

Stencilling Country Style

Bramble
BORDER

Weave a tangle of autumn leaves and berries in a continuous border to lend rustic charm to any room. Blended stencil colors look complicated but are simple and as quick as one-color work—all you need are brushes, water-based stencil paints and the bramble border stencil.

A border is a wonderfully versatile decoration, and you can use this pretty repeating leaf-and-berry pattern in any combination of colors to decorate walls, furniture or accessories. Our two examples show how you can use autumn colors to give a country look to a kitchen or family room and sophisticated mauves and grays to complement an elegant dining room or a bedroom.

Color blending

Choose water-based stencil paint in colors to match an element in your curtains or upholstery. You can be as imaginative as you like—there is absolutely no need to be realistic. Select three or four colors that look good together, making sure that there is sufficient difference in tones between them to make an interesting contrast. Pour a little of each paint into a saucer, plastic plate or palette and practice picking up a little of each in turn on a clean brush and dabbing it on plain white paper, seeing what effects you get when each color is blended next to the others. To be extra sure, attach your stencil to the sheet of

39

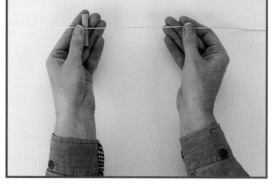

paper and test the colors together, planning which areas you want to stencil in which colors. The aim is to use two or more colors within each cutout of the stencil, so dab in small areas of each different paint and experiment half-covering areas that are already stenciled, using different colors. For convenience, use one brush for each color.

Planning

Just as when applying a wallpaper border, proper planning is essential. We'll show you a clever way to mark a straight line to follow, show you how to repeat the motif and also give you tips about carrying the pattern around corners—all the tricks you need to give your stenciling a really professional finish.

1 Perfect straight lines

● Before you start stenciling, mark the whole room with guidelines. Plan the line that will be the mark on which you position the bottom of the stencil; mark this point with colored chalk at one end of your wall and measure how far it is from the top of the

baseboard. Measure this same distance upward from the baseboard at the other end of the wall and mark with chalk. Depending on how solid your walls are, attach a pushpin or thumbtack to a length of thin cord and tap it lightly into the wall at one end of the room.

2 Marking the cord

● Gradually unwind the cord, running it over a piece of colored chalk in your hand so that it is completely coated. Keep unrolling the cord until you reach

the mark at the other end of the wall, then make a knot and keeping the cord taut, pin it to the mark. Check the cord with a level to be sure that it is perfectly even.

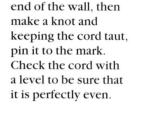

3 Instant guidelines

● Taking care not to pull the pins out of the wall, gently lift the cord away from the wall and allow it to twang back. The impact of the cord hitting the wall will leave a perfectly straight chalk line. Repeat the procedure across all the walls you intend to stencil.

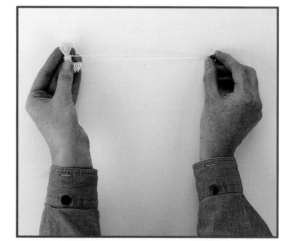

E Q U I P M E N T

PHOTOGRAPHY BY LIZZIE ORME

YOU WILL NEED:
● **Bramble border stencil, p. 103-112**
● **2-oz bottles of water-based stencil paint in green, red and gold**
● **Paint in background color**
● **Three medium-sized stencil brushes (size 6 or 8)**
● **Artist's brush**
● **Tape measure**
● **Colored chalk**
● **Two pushpins**
● **Fine cord or twine the length of the longest wall**
● **Masking tape**
● **Plastic plate or palette**
● **Plain white paper**
● **Firm cardboard**
The above quantities are sufficient for a border around a 12' x 15' room.

4 Position the stencil

● For the first pattern of the border, start about 4" away from one corner of the room. Choose a corner where a join will be least visible or that will be hidden by a curtain. Position the stencil with the bottom edge of the acetate just on the guideline. Secure it using masking tape or low-tack spray adhesive.

5 Stencilling the first colour

● Load your brush with a little of the first color (green) and dab off excess paint. Dab the paint on in an up-and-down (pouncing) motion, covering the stems, the outside edges of the larger leaves and the smaller sprigs. Set aside the brush and paint.

6 The second colour

● Using a fresh brush, pick up the red paint and stencil as before, covering the berries and rosehips. If you like, use a small piece of cardboard to mask areas where you do not want to overlap the colors.
● With very little paint remaining on the brush, dab very lightly over some areas of the stems and parts of the leaves. The goal is to give a shading of color all over with no large areas of solid color. Set aside the brush and paint.

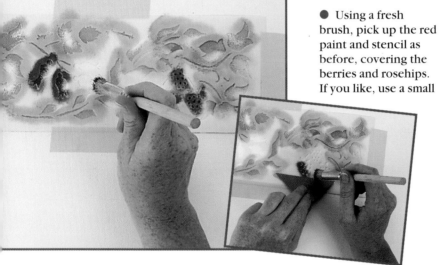

● Try decorating accessories using the border in different colors. Cool mauve, gray and purple give an elegant look to a plain straight-sided wastebasket. Choose colors to match fabrics or carpets for a coordinated look.

ADRIAN TAYLOR

HELP FILE

CORNERS
Attach the end of the stencil to the wall, matching the previous motif, and tape in place close to the corner. Press a piece of cardboard into the angle and tape in place on the other side of the angle. Still holding the cardboard, stencil the first side; when the paint is dry, stencil the other side in the same way.

UNEVEN WALLS
If your walls are asymmetrical and vary in height, do not place a border near the ceiling as this will accentuate the defect. Instead, position the border in the middle of the wall, taking a constant measurement upward from the floor or baseboard.

UNEVEN CORNERS
If your room does not have perfect 90° corners, make sure the stencil stays on the marked guideline and loosen it on one side of the corner as you stencil the other side of the angle. Re-attach the second side and loosen the first to match up the design.

! Never skimp on preparation—it is vital to mark a line for the border so that you have an established constant. Measure a set distance from the ceiling or baseboard, whichever is more convenient; if you simply count on matching up to the last motif, you may compound any mistakes.

PHOTOGRAPHY BY LIZZIE ORME

7 The third color

● Finish the design with gold paint, filling in the remaining blank areas and dabbing lightly over areas on the leaves, berries and stems. Keep dabbing until you get the effect you want—after the first few complete patterns, you will get into an easy routine of coloring the different areas in your chosen colors.

TIPS

■ Water-based paint dries fast, so pour out only a little of each color at a time into your plastic plate, adding more as you need it.

■ If the paint tends to dry on your brushes between use, wrap the bristles in plastic wrap while you are working in other colors.

■ The signature of good stenciling is a sense of movement—a look that is lively and not flat. As you work, dab the paint so that it shades over into adjacent cutouts, giving the appearance of reflected color.

8 The second pattern

● Peel the masking tape away from the walls and when the first pattern is completely dry, reposition the stencil. The border is designed so that the last 1¼"-1½" exactly match the other end of the stencil; so to repeat the pattern, simply position the leaves at one end of the stencil over those you have already worked and reattach the stencil so that it rests as before along the chalk line.

9 Finishing touches

● Continue around the room, following the Help File on page 41 for stenciling around corners, until you reach the last corner. Work right up to the corner, then remove the stencil. Reposition it to match the very first motif, lining up the design exactly with the last one at the corner.

Stencil the last half motif, then remove the stencil. Touch up any smudges on the design using a little of the background paint and an artist's brush.
● Wipe away the chalk line with a clean cloth. Wash the brushes in warm soapy water and wipe the stencils clean with a damp cloth.

Border ideas

◀ Decorate a plain wooden cornice with a strip of bramble border in colors to coordinate with the drapery fabric or the painted woodwork.

▲ The bramble design is perfect to give a kitchen a rustic look—try it in a continuous strip on the backsplash between the base cabinets and wall cabinets.

◀ To work the border around a doorframe, mark a diagonal line in chalk coming out of each top corner of the frame. Stencil up to the first of these, not filling in beyond where you can see the line. Pivot the stencil around the corner and continue stenciling, taking care not to go beyond the chalk line.

▶ If stenciling over gloss paint, sand lightly so the paint will adhere and varnish over the dry stenciling.

▶ To use the stencil as a wallpaper, mark vertical lines at equal intervals along a wall below a chair rail and stencil in strips, as shown.

Wisteria

Create a charming floral frieze **with this** versatile wisteria **stencil design. With the clever use of** different shades of **color, you can give the beautiful climbing flowers a striking three-dimensional look.**

The magnificent hanging flowers, twining branches and delicate leaves of wisteria make it the perfect choice for a beautiful stenciled decoration. Take inspiration from the real thing—these glorious blooms can often be seen tumbling down the front of a house, framing the front door and windows. You can recreate this effect inside your home with stenciled leafy branches that ramble over a doorway or arch. Make a plain wisteria stem stencil to fit the dimensions of your door and use it as a "trunk" for the rest of the wisteria.

For a coordinated look, stencil flowers or leaves on pillows and curtains. Originally imported from the Far East, wisteria often appears as a motif on Oriental vases and ornaments, so you can even use your stencil as part of an Oriental theme.

Creating depth

To create the impression of masses of intertwined blooms with depth as well as height, experiment using light and dark colors and overlapping some of the motifs. Because pale colors recede and dark colors stand out, light green leaves will appear to be in the background while dark green leaves will seem to be in the foreground. Overlap a few leaves and flowers to add to the effect. Make sure the wall you are stenciling is a light, neutral color or you may lose the overall impression.

EQUIPMENT

YOU WILL NEED:
● Wisteria stencil,
p. 103-112
● Water-based stencil
paint in brown, white,
green, purple and mauve
● Large, medium-sized
and small stencil brushes
● Fine artist's brush
● Stencil acetate
● Plain white paper
● Pencil
● Scissors
● Masking tape
● Cutting mat or board
● Craft knife
● Palette or plastic plate

1 Draw a stem

● Using the plain paper and the
pencil, draw a wisteria stem about
7" x ½" to use as a linking stem.

Make sure your stem matches the
width of the stencil branch. The
shape should be slightly knobby to
match the rest of the branches.

2 Cut stencil acetate

● Using the scissors, cut a piece of stencil acetate that is slightly narrower than your sheet of paper.

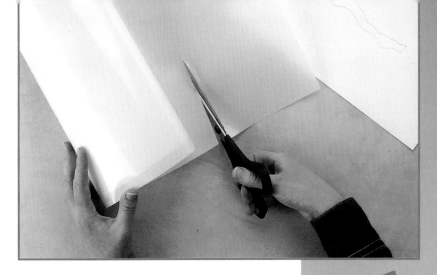

3 Trace the stem

● Place the acetate over your wisteria stem outline; using a sharp pencil, trace the shape. To stop the acetate from slipping, you can tape it to the surface on either side of the paper.

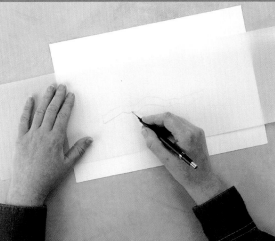

HELP FILE

■ If you overcut or tear your wisteria stem stencil while you are cutting it out, repair it with a small piece of masking tape trimmed to shape.

4 Cut your stencil

● Tape the acetate into position on the cutting mat, securing it at each edge. Using the the craft knife, carefully cut along the pencil outline of your wisteria stem.

5 Stencil the main stem

● With the medium-sized stencil brush and brown paint, stencil the stem. Then stencil the branch, overlapping the join. Continue stenciling, mixing branches and stems to form a main base.

■ You can cut stem stencils of two different lengths for your wisteria. Use the longer one just at the base of the arch or doorway to form a bare "trunk." Use the smaller stem mixed with the stencil branches to create the remainder of the base for your wisteria leaves and flowers.

47

6 Stencil the background leaves

● Using the medium-sized brush, stencil leaves using pale green paint. Position the leaves at any angle on both sides of the main stem. Leave room for the flowers and dark foreground leaves.

9 Peel away the stencil

● Carefully peel away the stencil to reveal a layered purple, mauve and white wisteria bloom.

7 Stencil all the flowers in white

● Using the large brush, stencil the wisteria flowers in white. All these blooms should hang from the underside of branches. Stencil the bud motifs in mauve.

8 Stencil flower in purple

● When the white paint has dried, reposition the flower stencil carefully over the top of a motif. With the small brush, stencil lightly in purple, adding a few touches of mauve.

11 Stencil the foreground leaves

● Place the leaf motif so that it overlaps a pale green background leaf or flower. Using the small or medium-sized brush, stencil in dark green.

10 Stencil the remainder of the flowers and buds

● Repeat steps 8 and 9 until all the wisteria flowers are complete. Add more wisteria buds in mauve or purple, without the white base coat.

■ Because you are working freehand rather than dabbing on colors through a stencil, dilute the paint for the wisteria tendrils (step 13) with a little water so it is easier to use.

■ If the pale green background leaves of your wisteria are too dark and there is not enough contrast between background and foreground leaves, lighten them with a little white stencil paint on an artist's brush.

■ When you are overlapping motifs, if the paint smudges and blurs with the colors underneath, let the motif dry completely and retouch later, using the fine artist's brush and stencil paint in the appropriate color.

■ Since the blooms of wisteria are quite similar to laburnum, try stenciling blossoms in two shades of yellow to create a completely different look.

■ If you feel confident painting freehand, there is no need to make your own stencil for the main trunk of the wisteria—paint directly on the wall using a medium-sized artist's brush. This will allow you scope to create curved, straight or twisted branches, according to the shape you want to achieve.

Wisteria pillow

For a coordinated look, stencil wisteria flowers and leaves on pillow covers. Choose fabric in a plain shade to contrast or blend with the base color of your wall. You don't have to stencil the wisteria flowers in lilac or purple—here we used yellow, bright green and white, with leaves in dark green, over a fabric in soft, pale green. For a simple but striking design, stencil just the leaf motif over plain fabric in the color used in your wall frieze. Team the pillow with curtains stenciled in the same design.

13 Paint in the tendrils

● Using the fine artist's brush and dark green paint, add thin wispy lines, running from branches or leaves and curling at the ends.

12 Stencil the rest of the foreground leaves

● Continue stenciling the foreground leaves, filling the spaces left in step 6. Stencil on both sides of the main stem. Overlap a few background leaves and some of the wisteria flowers.

!

For a three-dimensional effect, be careful not to overlap too many foreground leaves in a small area. This could make the overall effect look cluttered rather than three-dimensional.

Color guide

Real wisteria blooms may be just shades of purple, but when you're creating your own, the color combinations are limitless. Choose colors to suit existing decor—for example, bright red flowers work well with green leaves on a white background to create a fresh look for a country-style kitchen. Blooms in fiery shades of yellow and orange are ideal with terra-cotta and brown, and bright blue on white is a good choice for a cool bathroom color scheme.

Sweet peas

Create a fresh new look for a room with this pretty sweet pea stencil. Versatile and simple to use, **the floral motif is perfect for trying out the technique of color blending.**

Use this sweet pea stencil to create a colorful vine design for your walls. You can add curtains or a tablecloth in a matching pattern to complete a pretty new look for a room. The stencil is easy to use on both walls and fabric, and because a casual, random arrangement of the motifs works best, there's no need for any time-consuming measuring and marking.

Color blending

The sweet pea motif lends itself to strong, natural colors. Deep purples, pinks and vivid greens are ideal. Flower designs are wonderful for experimenting with color blending. Different shades of paint can be placed next to each other on petals or stalks and blended together. It's easy to do, and the finished look is natural and vibrant. Just as nature creates flowers and plants that are dappled with a variety of colors and shades, so you can use this stencil to achieve similarly stunning effects indoors.

Sweet pea wall stencil

The sweet pea stencil is very versatile, so however you position it, the results should look good. You can stencil around all four walls of a room or just concentrate on the corners of the room, as in the picture above. A simple corner effect can give the prettiest look if you are making matching curtains or slipcovers as well.

Prepare your surface by making sure the wall is clean. Wash the wall with a mild household cleaner, then allow it to dry completely.

STENCIL PAINT FROM THE STENCIL STORE

1 Position the first stalk

● Position the stencil for the first stalk motif at the base of the wall just above the baseboard with the stalk facing directly upward. Stencil the stalk in green.

TIPS

■ Don't worry too much if the colors from the flowers and the stems bleed into each other. It makes the design look more natural. Real flowers don't always have a sudden cutoff point between where the green of the stem finishes and the colors of the petals start to appear.

■ You can place separate flowers so that leaves overlap petals and vice versa. This adds to the natural feel.

■ You can omit one or two of the petals from some of the flowers for variety.

■ When you are using a sponge, be careful to dab off the excess paint before you put it on the stencil.

2 Place the second stalk

● After you have stenciled the first stalk, move the stencil up so that a second stalk connects with the first, creating one long stalk.

3 Join stalks

● Continue stenciling the stalks up the wall so that each new stalk is lined up with the one below. You are aiming for a vine effect, so the stalks need to look as though they're joined but don't need to be in a perfectly straight line. Try not to use the same shade of green all along the stalk. Different shades give the plant movement.

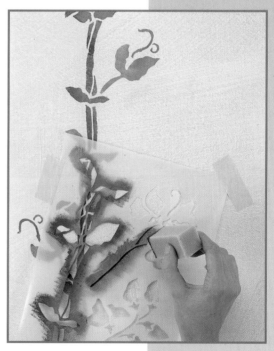

YOU WILL NEED:

● Sweet pea stencil (see pages 103-112)
● Water-based stencil paint in green, white, bright and soft pink, purple and yellow
● Household sponge or foam sponge, cut into pieces
● Masking tape
● Palette or plastic plate

4 Add leaves and tendrils

● Once you have stenciled the main stalk, going as far up as you want it to go, start adding the leaves and the delicate tendrils at random intervals. Stenciling the fine tendril areas can be a bit tedious, so try cutting your sponge into smaller pieces or use a small paintbrush to make it easier.

5 Start the first flower

● Place the fine stem of the first flower toward the base of the main stalk. The paint on the stalk and tendril area should be dry by now, so don't worry about putting the stencil on top of these. Just make sure that you don't stick the masking tape on any painted areas, or the paint may lift off when you peel away the tape.

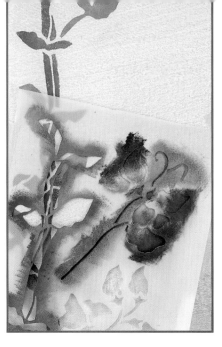

7 Final blending

● Add a lighter shade to the inside of the petal and work toward the center so that it blends in with the darker shade. If you need any extra help with blending, use a clean dry small piece of sponge or a small brush and gently dab the paint in the middle of the petal.

6 Color the petals

● Place a dark shade of your chosen color on the outside edge of the petal and work toward the center with your brush or sponge. Don't use the same shade across the whole petal as this will make it look too flat. Blended shades of the same color or of similar colors give a far more interesting and natural look.

8 Flip the stencil

● Place a sweet pea on the other side of the stalk by flipping the stencil. Make sure the underside of the stencil is clean and dry before you do this or you may mark the wall.

9 Work upward

● Work your way up the stalk, adding more stems and petals on either side. There's no need to position any parts of the plant symmetrically; the more random the placement, the more natural it will look. Stencil a few sweet peas so that they appear to grow out of the stems of other flowers, rather than out of the main stalk.

Sweet pea curtains

■ You don't need as much fabric paint on your brush as you would with ordinary paints, so be cautious with quantities, especially if you are mixing your own colors. Dab the paint on thinly, building up the color gradually.

■ Some standard water-based paints can be used on fabrics. Check with the manufacturer's instructions.

■ The sweet pea design is ideal for randomly-placed motifs, but try not to clutter the flowers by stenciling them too close together.

■ Fabric paint isn't colorfast until it has been heat-set—so if you make a mistake, you can gently rub off the paint with a clean damp cloth and stencil over again.

■ If you are stenciling a wall, and paint seeps under the edges of the stencil, wait until the paint is dry, then use a small fine-tip brush and a little of the background paint to cover up the smudged edge. Likewise, if you decide you don't like the position of a motif, paint over it with the background color.

■ Different fabric paints are available for use on cotton, silk and synthetics. Make sure you pick the paint most suited to your fabric type.

Stenciling on fabric is simple—and using the sweet pea stencil to decorate a pair of curtains is especially straightforward. You don't even need to worry about positioning the motifs geometrically; because of the folds in curtain fabric, you won't be able to see any precise positioning anyway once you hang the curtains. One of the important points to remember about stenciling on fabric is that you need to secure the fabric firmly to your work surface and keep it taut. You also need to place some shirt cardboard under the fabric while you are stenciling.

EQUIPMENT.

YOU WILL NEED:

● Sweet pea stencil (see pages 103-112)
● Fabric paints in sweet pea colors
● Fabric paint crayons (optional)
● Stencil brushes
● Fabric
● Thin shirt cardboard
● Masking tape
● Palette

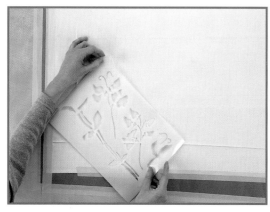

1 Position the stencil

● To stencil a row of sweet peas along the bottom of the fabric, start by ironing a crease where you want the base of the row to appear. Leave a reasonable gap between the crease and the edge so that you can hem the fabric. Position the stencil of the first sweet pea so that the base of the stalk rests on the ironed crease.

2 Start to color

● Pour a small amount of each of your chosen colors into a palette. Pick up a small amount of the color you are using for the stem on the end of your brush, then dab off the excess. You can use any stencil brush, but we used a special fabric stencil brush for our sweet peas. This has longer bristles, which you may find easier to use.

! Place a piece of shirt cardboard or plastic-covered cardboard under the fabric while you are stenciling, so that paint can't seep through to the other side and your work surface is protected. Secure the cardboard with masking tape and place the fabric on top, securing this with masking tape as well so that it remains taut.

4 Add more motifs

● Continue stenciling the flowers along the crease line and upwards. Don't worry too much about the distance between each flower but try to vary the direction and the angle of the flowers by flipping the stencil as you work your way across the fabric.

● It's important to use a fresh piece of cardboard each time you lift the fabric. Wet paint from the old piece can mark the underside of the fabric.

3 Finish the first flower

● Sweet peas are bright, vibrant flowers so you can be quite bold with the colors you choose for the petals. But be careful with the amount of paint you put on the brush— fabric paint colors tend to be stronger and more vivid than ordinary paint colors.

Using fabric paint crayons

● If you want to try something a bit different, use fabric paint crayons to make dots, squiggles and other similar effects.

Spring flowers

In a pretty bedroom, a scattering of stenciled violets adds a special charm. Discover how to stencil with a brush in two colors and create an allover wall pattern with a random stenciling of spring flowers and smaller sprigs.

A dainty design deserves delicate colors. Blend stencil paints for the leaves and petals in colors that complement the color scheme in your room—that's the beauty of using stencils as designer wallpaper!

YOU WILL NEED:
- Spring flowers stencil (see pages 103-112)
- One or two 2-oz bottles each of water-based stencil paint in soft green and dusky pink
- Two stencil brushes (size 4 or 6)
- Saucers or a palette
- Paper towels
- Plain white paper
- Masking tape or low-tack spray adhesive

Today, as more people want to stamp an individual style on their homes, the stencil is proving its versatility as a decorative effect. For centuries craftsmen all over the world used stencils to add elegance and detail to the walls of churches, palaces and mansions—then, in the postwar paper shortages, stenciling became popular as a cheap alternative to wallpaper. Now, however, stenciling has regained its status as an art form, and modern paints and equipment make it easy to express your individuality with a variety of specially created designs.

Starting from scratch

If you are stenciling for the first time, a random spriggy design, such as these violets, provides an ideal introduction. In this cottagey bedroom, we have used one main stencil and two small sprigs to cover the walls all over in a delicate pattern. The overall effect may look ambitious, but because the positioning of the stencils is completely random, and the designs are done in easy-to-use water-based stencil paints, it is easy to make the two-color motifs perfect every time.

Equipment for stenciling

As you gather together your equipment, select stencil paint in colors that will blend comfortably with the look and feel of your room. If you cannot find a ready-mixed color that fits the bill, buy a selection of colors and blend your own paint. Remember, if you do this, to mix a large enough quantity to deal with the whole job, as it is often difficult to recreate an exact shade if you run out.

Because the flower stencil has very fine bridges, it is easiest to stencil the design using a brush—having one brush for each color will save washing between different paints. Brushes come in a range of sizes, but for work on a delicate design, you need nothing larger than a size 6.

Making and using stencils

Use one of the two methods described on page 103 to trace and cut a stencil out of durable stencil acetate. Although you can use card stencils, they do not last as long and are more difficult to position accurately and to keep clean.

Stenciling with a brush is a vertical movement, more like stippling than brushing. Practice the technique on a sheet of plain white paper (see steps opposite) and test to see how much or how little paint you need to get the best effects. Provided you dip only the very tips of the bristles in the paint, you can dab or stipple with quite a firm up-and-down (pouncing) motion without fear of smudging the edges.

Remember—stenciling is fun, and even if you find that the paint has smudged, it is always easy to correct flaws when the stencil paint has dried—so you can afford to be confident and experiment with textures and colors.

1 Preparation

- Whether you are going to stencil directly onto an existing painted surface or paint a room from scratch, you will need to remove any traces of grease or dirt from the walls before you can start. Both stencil paints and latex paints need a clean base to adhere to.
- Wash walls starting from the bottom upward, using a warm solution of a mild household cleaner, then let the walls dry completely. If you want to paint the walls, choose a matte-finish latex, which gives an ideal surface for stencil paints to adhere to. Cover with one or two coats using a brush or roller; let the walls dry completely before stenciling.

EQUIPMENT

PHOTOGRAPHY BY GRAHAM RAE

2 Brush test

● Pour a little stencil paint into a saucer and dip just the tip of the brush in it to coat the ends of the bristles completely. When you start, it is easy to load the brush with too much paint, which will make your stenciling look thick and untextured.

● Dab the end of the brush on a paper towel to get rid of any excess paint and to distribute the paint evenly over the ends of the bristles. This exercise will also help you gauge the effect that you will get when you start stenciling and prevent you from smudging paint under the bridges.

Check with the manufacturer's instructions to find out if their brand of stencil paints will adhere to shiny surfaces, such as gloss paint or laminates. Water-based paints adhere easily to porous non-oil-based surfaces but will need protective varnishing if they are to be used on ceramics or similar surfaces.

3 Stencil test

● Test your technique before you start stenciling. Place the stencil on a piece of plain white paper and begin to color it in, holding the brush at right angles to the paper and using a pouncing motion. You will see the effects that come from using different amounts of paint on your brush.

● Wipe the stencil clean with a damp cloth and pat it dry with a paper towel. You need to start stenciling from one corner of the room, so position the stencil for

your first motif where you want to start and attach it to the wall, using a piece of

masking tape on each edge or low-tack spray adhesive to stop it from slipping. Do not use ordinary adhesive tape, as this may lift the base paint.

■ If you realize you have filled in an area in the wrong color, make sure the paint is completely dry to avoid blending colors, then stencil over the top in the right color.

■ You may find, when you lift the stencil off the wall, that you have not filled in some areas enough. Reposition the stencil carefully, tape it in place and stencil over the area again— stenciling is easy to alter or repair.

■ If, when you stand back from the finished effect, you are not happy with the placement of any of the motifs, you can paint right over a "mistake" when the stencil paint is dry, using one or two coats of the background paint color.

● Use your stencil to add detail to accessories. This tray, painted in white enamel, has been decorated with a single motif, then varnished to give a protective coating.

4 Stenciling

● With your stencil in position on the wall, load your brush with green paint and dab off the excess on a paper towel. Use the brush in a light, up-and-down dabbing motion to color in the stems and leaves. Build up the color from a light shading to a more solid cover—if you use just a little paint, you can gradually add more, avoiding making blobs of paint that may smudge when you remove the stencil.

● Keep the stencil taped in position and load a second brush with dusky pink paint. Wipe off the excess as before, then fill in the flowers and buds. Water-based paints dry quickly, so you are unlikely to smudge the green if you accidentally brush pink onto it. For better control in areas where the bridges between areas of different colors are thin, tilt the brush slightly so that you are using just one side of the bristles. The more you use them, the more flexible stenciling brushes become, making them easier to use selectively for fine stenciling.

PHOTOGRAPHY BY GRAHAM RAE

■ To give a gentle, random effect, intersperse the two small sprigs on the stencil between the larger clusters, allowing plenty of space around each motif to prevent the pattern from looking cluttered.

■ For additional variety, clean the stencil thoroughly and flip it over before repositioning it on the wall to create a reversed motif.

■ The flower stencil has a versatile design, and you can use small areas of it as sprigs or single stems. Use masking tape on the back of the stencil to block off areas you do not want to use before repositioning it on the wall. You can also do this if you are stenciling small areas of color with thin bridges.

5 Repeat motifs

● When you have completed both colors on the motif, remove the masking tape, peeling it back gently from each edge. Lift the stencil straight off to avoid smudging and wipe it clean with a damp cloth. Choose where you want to stencil the next motif, remembering to use small sprigs among the larger motifs—without these, the effect would become monotonous.

6 Final touches

● No matter how careful you are, paint can seep slightly under the edges of the stencil. To remedy this, wait until the paint is completely dry, then use an artist's brush and a little background paint to paint over the smudged edge.

● When you have finished stenciling, place the stencil on a flat surface and clean with a damp cloth. Work inward toward the center of the design—you will find that you do not need to press hard to remove the paint. Clean along stems and thin areas so as not to tear the bridges.

The flower motif is effective stenciled in different color combinations or all in one color.

● Use this versatile flower motif to add charm to accessories in a stenciled room—stencil a border of sprigs around a plain paper lampshade or add a motif to a bedside table. A whole room decorated with allover stenciling like this is best done in gentle, muted colors over a light background, but single motifs can look spectacular on a darker background in bolder, contrasting colors. You do not need to stick to traditional violet colors—the flower motif looks charming in fantasy colors, as shown in these examples.

Garden

Transform your kitchen with a crop of
vegetable motifs—stenciled in colorful shades
on walls, baseboard, linens or ceramics, they
look good enough to eat.

vegetables

Succulent mushrooms, plump peas in their pods, freshly picked asparagus and delicious corn on the cob all add up to a mouth-watering vegetable feast—and the perfect decorating theme for any kitchen. Stenciled in a repeat pattern over a painted grid, they give the look of expensive hand-painted tiles but at a fraction of the cost! Use all the vegetable motifs or select just a couple of them; stencil in each grid square or leave some plain—the possibilities are endless.

Stenciled accessories

For a striking finishing touch, stencil the motifs on a faux baseboard painted in a bright color to contrast with the rest of your garden vegetable wall. Use just the pea pod motif or add groups of two or three of the vegetables, stenciled all around the baseboard.

The motifs also make ideal decorations for ceramic bowls, plates or containers, or you can use them on fabrics, adding a border to plain tablecloths and napkins.

YOU WILL NEED:

- **Vegetable stencil, p. 103-112**
- **Water-based stencil paints in sea green, emerald, yellow, white and light brown**
- **Flat latex paint in cream and terra-cotta**
- **Medium-sized paintbrush**
- **Medium-sized artist's brush**
- **Plumb line**
- **Tape measure**
- **Ruler**
- **Pencil**
- **Scissors**
- **Masking tape**
- **Paint pail**
- **Measuring cup**
- **Mixing spoons**
- **Low-tack spray adhesive**
- **Foam sponge or household sponge**

1 Mark out the grid

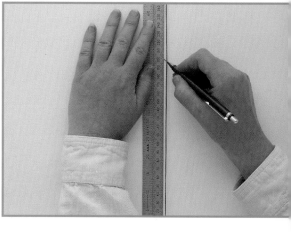

- Apply a coat of cream latex paint to the wall. Let dry for 2–4 hours. Suspend the plumb line 8" from the corner of the wall and mark 8" intervals along its drop, starting at the baseboard level and working up so as to create a whole "tile" at the bottom. Continue across the walls at 8" intervals.

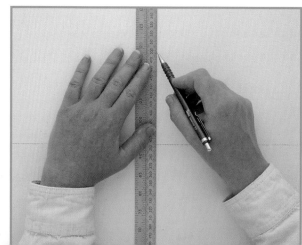

2 Draw in the lines

- With the ruler and pencil, connect the marks to form a grid. Mark the horizontal lines first, then the vertical.

3 Mask off "tile" squares

● Mask off strips about ¼" wide over the horizontal grid lines. (For an alternative, see Tips, page 67.)

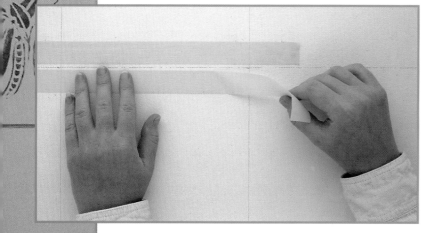

4 Paint the grid

● Pour a little terra-cotta latex paint into the paint pail and dilute with twice as much water. Using the medium-sized artist's brush, paint the masked-off area. Repeat steps 3 and 4 over the vertical lines, allowing the paint to dry before remasking for the verticals.

5 Plan the pattern

● Starting at the top left-hand corner of the wall in the first square of the row, place the asparagus motif carefully at a slight angle across the center. Draw the outline lightly in pencil. Leave the next square blank, then position and draw in the mushroom. Moving to the row below, leave the first square blank, draw an outline of the pea pod in the next, skip a square and then draw in a second pea pod motif.

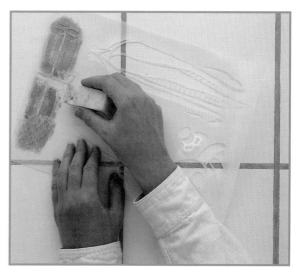

6 Stencil the first motif

● Position the asparagus motif over the pencil guidelines, securing with spray adhesive. Using small pieces of sponge, stencil in sea green and emerald, working over the pencil marks and blending the two colors. Stencil the ribbon in yellow.

7 Complete the pattern

● Stencil the pea pod motifs in sea green and yellow and the mushrooms in brown and white. This pattern of motifs forms the basis of your repeat design. Work over four columns at a time, continuing until you have filled in all the alternate spaces of the grid.

Baseboard motifs

If your kitchen has no baseboard, create one with paint, then add a finishing touch with a border of stenciled vegetables to coordinate with your stenciled walls.

YOU WILL NEED:
- Garden vegetable stencil, p. 103-112
- Flat latex paint in terra-cotta
- Water-based stencil paint in brown
- Natural sponge
- Foam sponge or household sponge, cut into pieces
- Ruler
- Tape measure
- Pencil
- Scissors
- Masking tape
- Low-tack spray adhesive

1 Mark the pencil guidelines

● Using the ruler, tape measure and pencil, measure up 4¾" from the floor and make marks at intervals along the rest of the walls.

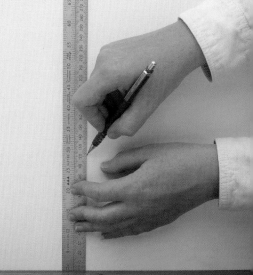

2 Draw in the baseboard

● Using the pencil and ruler, draw a straight line to connect the marks. This line marks the top of the "flat" area of the baseboard.

If you are combining this baseboard effect with the vegetable "tiles," mark the height of the baseboard before you plan the tile grid and work upward from here to avoid making half tiles at the bottom.

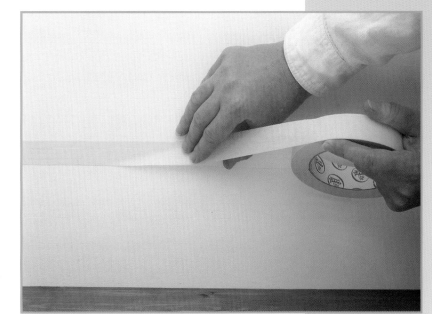

3 Mask off the baseboard

● Mask off the pencil guideline, positioning the tape along the top of the marked pencil line.

4 Mask off parallel line

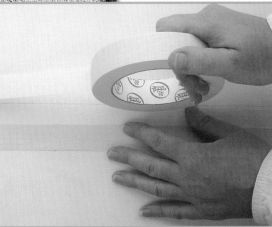

● Measure ¾" from the top of the tape and mark at intervals. Connect the marks and position a strip of masking tape above this line to give a masked-off ¾" strip parallel to and above the baseboard.

5 Sponge on paint

● Using the natural sponge, dab the terra-cotta latex paint over the flat baseboard area and masked-off line. Let dry for 2–4 hours. If you are working above a carpeted area, either cover it with a drop cloth or fold back the carpet before you start.

6 Stenciling

● Remove the masking tape and place the pea pod motif over the sponged baseboard—the top of the pea pod should just overlap the plain cream stripe above. Secure with spray adhesive and stencil, using the foam sponge and brown paint. Repeat along the rest of the baseboard.

TIPS

■ To create a soft, dappled background on your stenciled baseboard, dampen the sponge slightly with water before you start dabbing on the terra-cotta paint.

■ For added realism, load a small brush with diluted terra-cotta paint, wipe off the excess and draw the brush horizontally along the plain strip of the baseboard to give a light dragged effect.

■ When you are marking the grid for your stenciled wall, as you are starting at the bottom, you may have incomplete squares at the top of the wall. If so, start stenciling in the first row of complete squares.

■ As an alternative to masking off and painting on the grid, you can use a stencil instead. Simply draw a line ¾" wide and 8" long on stencil acetate and cut it out using a craft knife.

Willow pattern

The fashion for displaying blue-and-white china dates from the Victorian era. You can carry on the tradition by stenciling this beautiful willow-patterned plate, cup and saucer as a trompe l'oeil effect on a plain wall.

YOU WILL NEED:
- Willow pattern stencil, p. 103-112
- 1-oz bottles of stencil paint in medium blue, dark blue and gray
- White latex paint
- Small and medium-sized stencil brushes
- Fine artist's brush
- Wide artist's brush
- Scissors
- Masking tape
- Palette or saucer

China has always been a popular choice with collectors and one of the best loved designs is the blue-and-white Chinese-style willow pattern. This plate, cup and saucer stencil takes its inspiration from the traditional design and can be used on walls to create a decorative trompe l'oeil effect, which mimics the real thing. The stencil looks complicated, but because just one main color is used with two highlight shades, it is simple to create and the results are striking. Line up the stencils above a display rail or repeat the pattern above a shelf as a backdrop to your own collection of blue-and-white china.

Stencil crayons

Solid stencil paint crayons look exactly like children's wax crayons. To use them, you rub them on a stencil blank or a piece of shirt cardboard, which you then use to load your brush from, like an artist's palette. Stencil crayons are very quick and easy to use—however, they take slightly longer to dry than liquid stencil paints. Stencil crayons are available in a wide range of colors, including gold and silver, but you can also mix your own colors. Stencil crayons and stencil paints produce the same effect, so you can try both and choose which you prefer.

1 Prepare the stencils

- Although you could use the plate and cup stencils joined together, it is easier to separate them. Cut between the two motifs; to extend the stencils, stick an over-lapping strip of masking tape along the cut edge of both pieces. Turn over and cover with another strip on the reverse.
- Place the lower edge of the plate stencil at the top of the display rail and hold in place with masking tape. Make a pencil line through the bottom of the stencil and check that it is close enough to the rail. When you are happy with the position, secure at the top corners and above the rail.

2 Fill in the first color

- Pour a little medium blue paint into a palette and use the medium-sized brush to dab it over the entire stencil design. Where the stencil juts over the display rail, hold it flat against the wall with the fingers of your free hand as you work. Allow to dry, then add shading with the dark blue stencil paint.

3 Touching-up

- Peel the stencil away from the wall and check to see if there are any areas that need touching-up—this probably will happen at the base of the plate where the stencil is not held firmly against the wall. When the stencil paint is dry, use a fine artist's brush and the white background latex paint to even out any areas where the paint has smudged.

4 Add the saucer

- Position the saucer stencil where you would like it to sit above the display rail, checking that it sits on the rail at the same level as the plate. Secure it in position with masking tape. As for the plate, use the medium blue stencil paint to fill in the whole design, then allow to dry.

5 Apply the second colour

- Use the dark blue paint to add shading on the cup and saucer, applying it to the inside of the cup under the bottom of the saucer with the smaller stencil brush. Peel the masking tape from the wall and remove the stencil. Touch up any smudged edges as before.

6 Add a hand-painted shadow

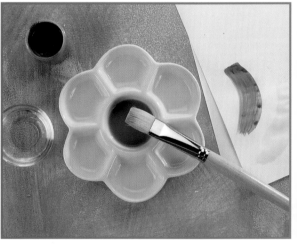

- To get the three-dimensional look of a plate resting against a wall, add a hand-painted shadow. Dilute a little gray paint with water to make it look more translucent. Test this color on a piece of scrap paper using a wide artist's brush—the aim is to get a soft gray tone. If the color appears too dark, add a little more water. If it is too light, add a little more gray paint.
- Working to one side of the plate, paint in a soft-edged shadow. Start at the bottom of the plate, keeping the line the width of the brush. Continue the line around to the top of the plate in one even brushstroke.

Stencil Crayons

An alternative to liquid stencil paints, crayons are a simple, effective stenciling medium. They are suitable to use on many surfaces, from furniture to walls.

Mark the background

- If you are stenciling on a colored wall, first paint a white circle as a background. Place the plate stencil on the wall and tape with masking tape. Draw around the outside of the plate along the four solid rim sections only. Carefully pull stencil off the wall.
- Keeping the center point of the stencil in contact with the wall, rotate the design by a quarter turn to the right. The

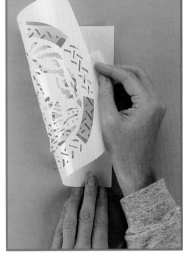

four solid rim sections of the plate are now positioned at different intervals along the circumference of the outer edge.
- Using masking tape, reposition the stencil and draw along the solid outer rim lines as before. Remove the stencil and complete the circle by filling in the broken arcs. Or use a plate the same size to draw an outline.

! Stencil crayons self-seal after use, but you can help keep them from drying out by wrapping them in plastic wrap. Store flat in a container with a tight-fitting lid. As these crayons are made from oil-based colors, you will need to clean your brushes with paint thinner after use. Wipe stencils clean with a cloth dampened with paint thinner.

1 Base coat

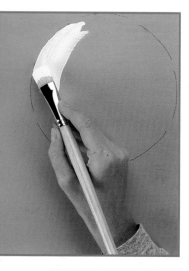

● Using the white latex paint as a base coat, apply the paint using a wide artist's brush and fill in the marked circle. Work in short, curved brushstrokes, starting at the outer edge of the circle and filling it in so that you finish in the center. Allow to dry for 2–4 hours, then rub away the pencil outline.

2 Position the stencil

● Making sure that the design of the stencil is perfectly straight, center it over the base coat circle so that the outer rim of the stencil matches up exactly with the edge of the white background. Fix the stencil in position on all four sides using masking tape.

3 Stencil crayons

● Break the protective seal by rubbing the end of the stencil crayon on a paper towel. Work a little color from the crayon onto a stencil blank; use this as a palette. Taking a clean stencil brush, work the bristles into the stencil color using a circular motion. Make sure the tip of the brush is completely covered with stencil color.

4 Stenciling

● Apply the deep pink color to the left half of the design in a dabbing motion, as for water-based paints, working from the outer edge toward the center. Gradually build up the depth of color you want by recovering the same area. Stencil crayon colors are less likely to bleed than water-based paints.

5 Blending

● Complete the stencil by filling in the right half with the bright red stencil color, blending the area where the two colors meet. This will give the effect of a light shadow cast across the surface of the plate. Remove the stencil very carefully— stencil crayon colors take about 12 hours to dry completely and can easily be smudged.

Finishing touches

Apply a gray shadow to the left side of the plate as in step 6 (page 70). Design your own rope-and-tassel stencil and position with a twisted cord above the plate and cord and tassels below. Stencil in white with gray highlights on top. Add a rosette at the top of the twisted cord.

Give your kitchen a touch of **farmhouse style** with handsome roosters and charming chicks and bring **a flavor of the countryside** into your home.

Rooster & chicks

Proud roosters in shades of red, brown and green, complete with their families of chicks, bring a farmhouse feel to a kitchen or family room. For added authenticity, stencil the rooster motif on plain cabinet doors and add a bed of straw using an improvised stamp—then cover with a square of chicken wire held in place with staples and molding.

Select the whimsical chick motifs to use on plain painted furniture or as a border above a chair rail or around a window. And for a finishing touch, stencil chicks and eggs on ceramic bowls and plates or on wooden accessories, such as kitchen stools, plant stands and window boxes.

Ceramic paints

These designs are perfect to use on ceramic surfaces—make sure you select a specialized ceramic paint or craft enamel and always follow the manufacturer's instructions carefully.

Depending upon the paint you select, you may need to bake the painted item to set the finish, so bear this in mind when choosing a bowl or plate to decorate and make sure the item will stand up to moderate oven heat.

PHOTOGRAPHY BY LIZZIE ORME

Roosters in coops

Transform plain cream-colored cabinet doors with these magnificent colorful roosters, complete with their own beds of straw and chicken-wire coops.

YOU WILL NEED:

- Rooster and chicks stencil (see pages 103-112)
- Flat latex paint in dark green
- Water-based stencil paint in brown, brick red, dark red, dark green, dark blue, brown, pale brown and yellow
- Metallic spray paint in copper
- Small and medium-sized paintbrushes
- Stencil brush
- Small artist's brush
- Chicken wire
- 4 yards of molding
- Ruler
- Scissors
- Corrugated cardboard
- Palette or plastic plate
- Masking tape
- Wire cutters
- Brown paper or newspaper
- Staple gun
- Pencil
- Miter box
- Saw
- Paint pail
- Mixing sticks
- Glue gun
- Glue sticks

1 Cut a strip of cardboard

- Cut a strip of cardboard roughly 1¼" wide and 8¾" long.

2 Bend the cardboard

- With the corrugated side down, bend the cardboard up in two places to form a U-shape with a flap on either side.

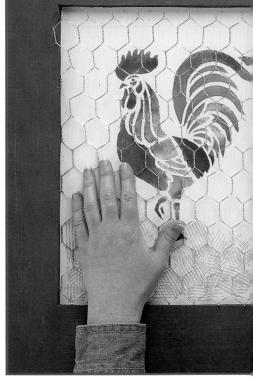

3 Paint the cardboard stamp

● Paint the frame area of the doors and rest of the cabinet in dark green flat latex paint. When dry, pour a little pale brown stencil paint into the palette. Using the small brush, apply paint to the corrugated base of the cardboard stamp.

4 Stamp the straw on the door

● If possible, remove the cabinet doors so that they are easier to work on. Dab the cardboard stamp at the base of the door in a crisscross pattern to create a straw effect. Make the bed of straw at least 2½" deep within the panel, as this will obscure the bottom of the cupboard (see step 12).

7 Cut the chicken wire to size

● Cut a piece of chicken wire a little smaller than your cabinet door. Press it against the door and, using the wire cutters, trim to fit the inside panel.

5 Position the stencil

● Pour a little of each of the remaining stencil paints into the palette. Position the rooster in the center of the door panel and secure with masking tape. Starting from the top, stencil in blended colors.

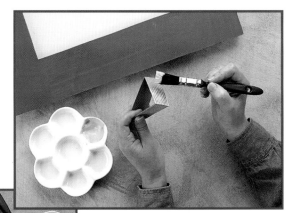

8 Spray chicken wire

● Place the cut chicken wire on a piece of brown paper and spray with the copper metallic paint. Apply the paint lightly, taking care not to clog the wire. Allow to dry for 30 minutes at the most.

6 Stencil the rooster

● Continue stenciling the rooster, using brick red and dark red for the comb, chin, back and legs, and dark green and dark blue for the tail feathers and breast. Stencil the rest of the rooster's feathers in brown, pale brown and yellow, adding a touch of red and blending colors at the edges. Allow to dry.

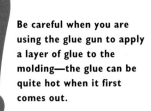

Be careful when you are using the glue gun to apply a layer of glue to the molding—the glue can be quite hot when it first comes out.

9 Secure the chicken wire

● Place the sprayed chicken wire over the door panel. Press it flat, pushing the wire firmly into the corners, and staple into place around each edge using a staple gun.

■ For blending large areas of color, such as the rooster's body, take a clean piece of sponge and dab it where two colors meet. This prevents the colors from becoming muddy.

■ Because the purpose of the molding is to obscure the edges of the chicken wire, you can use a narrow width as long as it conceals the staples.

■ Cut several cardboard stamps in varying lengths so that if the corrugated ridges become flat, you can use a fresh one.

■ If you prefer, use ordinary woodworker's glue instead of the glue gun.

■ If the staples holding your chicken wire seem loose, tap them lightly into place with a tack hammer.

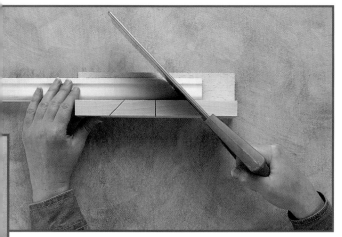

10 Cut the molding

● Measure the top and side of the cabinet panel and make a note of the figures. Mark the molding, measuring a length for each panel side plus the top and bottom. Place the molding in the miter box and align the first pencil mark with the first 45° saw guide; fit the saw blade into the slot and cut through the molding. Reposition the molding, aligning the second mark with the second 45° guide, and cut again. Repeat this process for the next three lengths.

11 Paint the molding

● Pour a little dark green flat latex paint into the paint pail and dilute with five times as much water, stirring continuously. Using the medium-sized paintbrush, paint the four pieces of molding and allow to dry.

12 Glue the molding

● Using the glue gun, coat the back of a length of molding with a line of glue and press in place. Repeat for the other three sides.

1 Plan the placement

● Using the china marker, mark positions for the chick and egg motifs around the bowl.

Chicks and eggs

Create a coordinated look for a variety of plain white ceramic dishes with pretty, newly hatched chicks stenciled in bright yellow, and delicate eggshells in pale shades of brown.

YOU WILL NEED:
● Rooster and chicks stencil
● Ceramic paint in green, yellow, brown, red and white
● Stencil brush
● Ceramic bowl
● China marker
● Scissors
● Masking tape
● Natural sponge
● Plastic plate or palette
● Scrap paper
● Low-tack spray adhesive

2 Mask off the base of the bowl

● Mask off a 1" border at the base of the bowl. Either cut small strips of masking tape or use flexible tape to accommodate the curve.

! Be sure to mark positions for all your chicks and eggs before you start stenciling or you may run out of space, leaving your bowl with an unsightly gap.

3 Prepare a piece of sponge

● Pull off a small piece of the natural sponge so that you have a piece that is the right size to use for stenciling.

4 Dab the sponge in paint

● Pour a little green ceramic paint on a plastic plate. Soften the sponge with a little water, then dip it into the paint. Dab off the excess on a piece of paper.

5 Sponge on the borders

● Dab the green paint on the masked-off border at the base of the bowl. If the bowl has a natural deep rim, you can use this as a guide to sponge on a second border at the top.

Plain wooden accessories, such as this bucket, provide ideal surfaces for a string of stenciled chicks. Color-wash the background a pale shade and use water-based stencil paints in yellows and oranges for the chicks. Add a coat of varnish to protect against wear and tear.

6 Stencil the chicks

● Pour a little of the yellow, brown, red and white paints on the plastic plate. Spray adhesive on the back of the stencil, then position the chick motif, using the marks as a guide. Using the brush, stencil the chick's body in yellow, with red for the beak and legs. Remove the stencil and position the egg motif near the chick. Press in place, then stencil in brown and white, blending the colors. Repeat around the bowl. To set the paint, bake the bowl in the oven according to the manufacturer's instructions.

■ Reposition the stencil carefully for each motif—because you are working on a curved bowl, it will be difficult to bend the stencil over a large area to stencil a chick and egg at one time.

■ For masking off a border around the bowl, you can use a flexible tape instead of making a curve with small strips of ordinary masking tape.

■ If you intend to stencil several ceramic bowls, you may find it easier to cut a second separate chick stencil without the rooster.

These designs for farm animals—cows, pigs, sheep and chickens—offer a quick and effective way to recreate the charm of traditional rustic painted furniture.

FARMYARD
animals

Whether you echo the theme of your kitchen and stencil these traditional country designs in monochrome shades or use realistic colors, these animal motifs add a distinctive simplicity to a kitchen or breakfast room.

One of the most effective uses of the animals is for an evenly spaced frieze on a plain white background set against a colored wall. The colors you choose are all-important in creating a look—the crisp contrast of delft blue and white is reminiscent of old-fashioned Dutch earthenware. Alternatively, you can use rustic browns and yellows for a warm country look, primary colors for a more naive appearance or simply pick out colors from the rest of your decor.

Painted furniture
Stenciling takes all the uncertainty out of painting furniture, with endless ready-made designs to use and results which are perfect every time. You get the most charming effects from stenciling over a base of flat latex paint—several coats of protective varnish will make the finish more durable.

Chest of drawers

Remove all handles and hardware, fill and sand any flaws in the finish, apply two coats of flat latex paint and your chest of drawers is ready for a complete transformation.

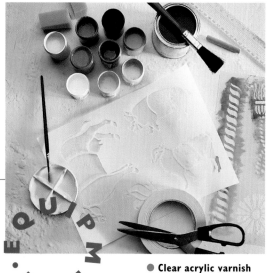

EQUIPMENT

YOU WILL NEED:
- Farmyard animals stencil (see pages 103-112)
- Stencil cut in a straight rope design
- Water-based stencil paints in chosen colors
- Clear acrylic varnish
- Fine artist's brush
- Brush for varnishing
- Ruler
- Chalk
- Scissors
- Masking tape
- Palette
- Household sponge or foam sponge, cut into pieces

1 Mark the drawer

● Using the ruler and chalk, mark the horizontal center of the drawer with a vertical line. Measure and mark the center points between this centerline and the position of the handles. Measure and mark the center point between the handle and the side edge of the drawer. Repeat this for all the drawers in turn.

2 Position the stencil

● Start with the cow stencil, because it is the largest and will determine the placement for the other stencils. Position the stencil squarely on the drawer so that the center of its body sits over the midpoint between the handle and the middle of the drawer. Fix in place with masking tape.

5 Draw grass tufts

● You can add tufts of grass freehand using a fine artist's brush, but if you prefer, draw your motif with an indelible marker on a small piece of stencil acetate. Cut it out on a cutting mat using a craft knife.

3 Mask the stencil

● Mask off the chicken stencil so there is no risk of dabbing color over that motif.

4 Stenciling

● Using realistic colors and the sponge, stencil the cow's feet, then blend the colors over the legs and body to give a natural look. When complete, remove the stencil, flip it over and, making sure the paint on it is dry, secure it in place on the other side of the drawer. Stencil as before.

6 Add grass

● Stencil or brush on tufts of grass around the feet of the cow. Remember that you can always touch up any small slips with the background color.

7 Varnish motifs

● Stencil a chicken motif over the center of the drawer. When dry, reposition the stencil over the motifs and apply a coat of varnish. Repeat steps 2 through 7 on the remaining drawers, using the other motifs and keeping them centered in line with the stenciled cows.

8 Rope border

● To create a rope frame, connect the chalk marks on the midpoint between the edge of the drawer and the handle with the drawers in place. Mark a top line on the frame of the chest above the top drawer and position a rosette stencil over the points where this joins the vertical lines. Position a rosette at the base of each vertical line and stencil the rope between them. If the chest is likely to have to withstand a lot of wear and tear, varnish the whole piece.

Decorated chair

YOU WILL NEED:

● Pig stencil, enlarged to fit chair, p. 103-112
● Artist's tube acrylics in bright shades to suit your room
● Clear acrylic varnish
● Stencil brushes
● Fine artist's brush
● Varnish brush
● Palette
● Water
● Craft sticks
● Scissors
● Masking tape

You do not need to use stencil paint when stenciling—use the vibrant, deep colors of artist's tube acrylics, which dry to a semi-gloss finish, to stencil and paint on a child's chair. Enlarge the motif by photocopying then recutting the stencil.

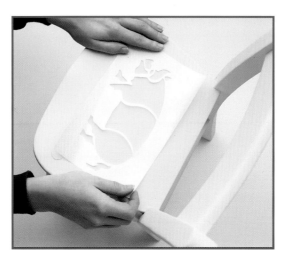

1 Prepare the colors

● Squeeze a small amount of artist's tube acrylic in the shade you have chosen for the pig into a small palette or mixing tray.

4 Positioning

● Decide where on the seat you want to place the stencil and secure it with masking tape. (When enlarging the stencil, gauge the size to fit on the seat with plenty of space all around.)

5 Stenciling

● Use diluted tube acrylics to stencil just as you would water-based stencil paint. Pick up the color on a stencil brush, dab off the excess on scrap paper and apply paint with a pouncing action.

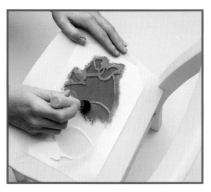

2 Dilute the color

● You will need to thin the acrylic color slightly to make it workable for stenciling. Add a few drops of water at a time, mixing until the consistency is like thick cream.

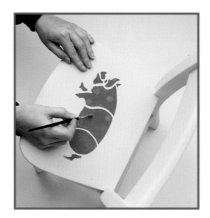

6 Add the spots

● When the paint is dry, use diluted tube acrylic in a contrasting shade to add spots with an artist's brush.

7 Add the highlights

● Use an even brighter color to add highlights over the spots.

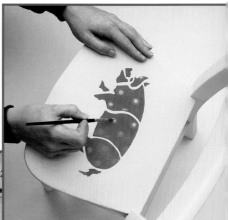

3 Combine colors

● If you have only primary colors, blend them together to create vibrant secondary colors, such as orange and purple. Mix a little at a time, because you will need to add water, as above, to get the color to the right consistency for stenciling and painting.

8 Finishing touches

● When the spots are dry, stencil the chair back with facing chickens. Use diluted tube acrylics in vibrant contrasting shades to add a wavy trim around the edge of the seat and down the back supports. Varnish the chair with clear acrylic varnish.

Rustic crockery

Combine elements of other rustic-style stencils in your collection with the farmyard animals to create different effects. The plate above uses the border from the Willow pattern design with the sheep stenciled in shaded delft blue in the center in place of the traditional Oriental scenes.

YOU WILL NEED:
- Sheep stencil and Willow pattern stencil, p. 103-112
- Water-based

- stencil paints in two shades of blue, and in white and green
- Fine artist's brush
- Scissors

- Masking tape
- Palette
- Household sponge or foam sponge, cut into pieces

1 Willow pattern border

- Mask off all the areas immediately next to the outer border of the Willow pattern plate, using masking tape. Use short pieces of tape so that you can mask off the design accurately.

2 Position stencil

- Position the stencil on the wall. If you are going to stencil more than one plate, you will need to measure and mark the wall with chalk or pencil so that they are positioned symmetrically and, if required, in a straight line.

3 Stenciling

- Using different shades of blue, stencil the border of the plate. Repeat as necessary.

4 Central motif

- Remove the plate stencil and when the paint is dry, center the sheep inside the border. Secure in place with masking tape.

5 Blended colors

- Stencil the sheep in shades of blue, blending in white to lighten the appearance. Take care not to stencil any of the other motifs.

6 Freehand touches

- Remove the stencil. When the paint is dry, use the green stencil paint and an artist's brush to add small tufts of grass around the feet of the sheep.

HELP FILE

■ Chests of drawers are often designed with drawers of varying depths. Number the drawers inside as you remove them to paint the background color so that you can plan which animals and motifs to put on which drawer.

■ If you are stenciling a selection of animals within a border panel, as on pages 80-81, make sure that they all appear to stand along a straight line. Make sure that the tallest animal you plan to use will sit symmetrically in the border, then mark a line at the level on which it is standing. If you prefer, use the chalk and string method, as detailed for the Bramble Border, page 40. Position the feet of all the animals along this line to give a neat constant along the base of the stenciling.

Alphabet

Add an individual touch to accessories and create your own personalized stationery with this versatile alphabet stencil—or use it to make a charming sampler.

3 Stencil the second and third lines

● Still using random colors, continue stenciling until you reach the end of the third line, finishing with the letter *T*. Remove the stencil.

Sampler

Create a charming, traditional sampler by stenciling directly onto embroidery cloth. The designs are worked in stencil paints, so there is no need to thread a single needle—although working over the textured fabric gives the stenciling a stitched appearance. Embellish the design with motifs, such as small animals or flowers, and create an alphabet or traditional "Home, Sweet Home" design. Plan the whole sampler on paper before you start—the threads of the fabric give you an easy guide to keep your letters in even rows.

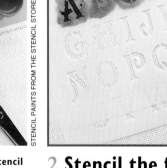

1 Tape stencil in place

● Tape the Aida cloth in place on a flat surface. Place the stencil on the Aida cloth according to your planned design and secure with masking tape.

4 Stencil the flower

● Select and mask off a flower motif and stencil it below the *Q*. Mask off a rabbit motif and stencil a facing rabbit on each side of the flower.

5 Stencil bottom line

● Remove the masking tape from the bottom line of alphabet letters. Tape this line into position under the rabbits and flower using top rows of letters as a guide. Stencil in random colors as for the other letters.

STENCIL PAINTS FROM THE STENCIL STORE

YOU WILL NEED:
● Alphabet stencil (see pages 103-112)
● Flower or animal stencils
● 14-count Aida cloth
● Water-based stencil paints in lilac, pink, purple, blue, white, yellow and green
● Stencil brush
● Scissors
● Masking tape

2 Stencil the first line

● Mask off the bottom line of letters on the stencil. With the brush, stencil the letters in the order they appear using a random color sequence.

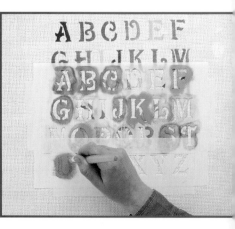

Candy jar

Transform plain glass storage jars in different shapes and sizes into a coordinated set with colorful stenciled names or initials. Use ceramic paints or craft enamels in colors to complement the contents of the containers—bright primary colors for a candy jar, shades of green for an herb jar or orange, green and cream for a pasta container. Before you start, make sure the container is large enough to accommodate the design you have chosen and plan how the letters will be spaced.

A B C D E F G H I J

1 Mask the jar

● Clean and dry the jar. Apply masking tape in a line at the top edge, just above where the stencil will sit.

2 Position the stencil

● Place the stencil so that it lies straight on the jar and smooth it. Tape it into place, pressing the masking tape onto the jar through the windows of the other alphabet motifs.

3 Stencil letters

● Using the brush and ceramic paint, stencil the first letter. Remove the stencil and allow the paint to dry. Reposition the stencil so that the second letter sits approximately $\frac{1}{8}$" to the right of the first. Stencil on another color. Continue, allowing paint to dry between letters, until you complete your planned name or initials.

YOU WILL NEED:
● Alphabet stencil, p. 103-112
● Ceramic stencil paint or craft enamel: one color for each letter
● Stencil brush
● Glass storage jar
● Scissors
● Masking tape

4 Peel off the tape

● Remove masking tape from the top edge of the jar.

TIPS

■ To avoid dabbing stray paint on the jar, mask off the letters around the one you are using.

■ Remember, the size of the jar will dictate how many letters you can use.

■ You can touch up any mistakes with ceramic paint and a fine artist's brush.

Stationery

Create your own personalized stationery, using the alphabet stencil and a clever airbrushing technique. All you need is a child's air art gun, available from hobby stores or mail-order catalogs, and a variety of brush-tip markers. Practice your technique with the art gun because the flow of ink can vary. Always start with the darkest color, airbrushing lighter colors over the top for a soft, mottled effect. Make sure that the paper stock you choose is not too glossy—if it is, the ink will not adhere. If you use initials rather than a whole word, you can stencil matching envelopes too. Use the technique on firm-textured wrapping paper to wrap personalized gifts.

YOU WILL NEED:

- **Alphabet stencil, p. 103-112**
- **Child's air art gun**
- **Air art-gun markers in green and yellow or desired colors**
- **Scissors**
- **Masking tape**
- **Paper and envelopes**

1 Undo the marker-holder

● Undo the screw in the art-gun marker-holder as far as it will go, taking care not to pull it out of the socket.

2 Insert marker

● Slide the green marker into the holder and tighten the screw. Make sure the nib of the marker sits right at the tip of the art-gun nozzle.

3 Stencil the first letter

● Mask off the letters around the one you are going to airbrush and tape the stencil in place. Color in the stencil by squeezing the bulb of the art gun in short, sharp blasts.

4 Airbrush in yellow

● Airbrush in yellow over the green letter.

TIPS

■ Use brown paper to protect your surface, as the ink can spray out over a large area.

■ Start with the darkest color—any light colors will be airbrushed out if you use them first.

■ Before you start, practice airbrushing on a piece of scrap paper.

Nursery corner frieze

The alphabet stencil is ideal for a children's room or nursery. Used on a plain wall, the letters are bright, bold and decorative—and you can use them to help your child learn the alphabet! Add a few stenciled motifs, such as butterflies, starfish, frogs and lambs, as a finishing touch. Use water-based stencil paints and add a coat of varnish to areas that are likely to get a lot of wear and tear.

These frogs are quick and simple to stencil—and add a charming splash of color, indoors or out. Learn how to blend water-based stencil paints with a sponge in easy-to-follow steps using these versatile motifs from the Stencil Designs pages.

Jumping FROGS

Stenciling is quicker, easier and less expensive than wallpapering—and even the simplest stencil can give the most charming effects.

Today the traditional art of stenciling is making a comeback and looks as if it is here to stay. With the endless variety of pre-cut stencils, specialized paints and colors available from art-supply stores, crafts shops and paint stores and by mail order, it has never been easier for even beginners to achieve professional-looking results.

Versatile decoration

With stenciling you can be as daring—or modest—as you like. You can add a single motif to transform something as small as a box or plan borders, details or even whole wall designs to give a room a new look. We have used the two frog motifs to give a touch of fun to a bathroom, a patio wall and a bench. There are no rules—sit a frog on a soap dish or arrange a group of frogs on an outdoor picnic table—stenciling is endlessly versatile.

Getting started

Stenciling is also simple, quick and above all fun to do—and satisfying results are easy to achieve. More than anything, when tackling your first project, remember that there is always a way to retouch a smudged edge (see

Finishing touches, page 96)—so you can afford to be confident.

Even if you are stenciling for the first time, you can be assured of good results if you follow the steps and work methodically. Before you start, assemble all the equipment you will need. For a first project, the most economical way to apply the water-based stencil paints used for the frog motifs is to use pieces of firm synthetic (household) sponge or foam sponge—this way you do not need to invest in stencil brushes and you can use a separate piece for each color of paint. Simply throw the sponge pieces away when you have finished.

Cutting the stencils

When making your own stencils, choose stencil acetate—a clear, durable plastic, so that the stencils are easy to clean and you can use them again and again. The clear acetate also gives you a good view for positioning the stencil.

To make the frog stencil, follow the instructions on page 103, and cut the design out of stencil acetate using a craft knife or a heat cutting tool.

When you finish any project, clean the stencil as shown on page 96, so it is ready to use another time, and store the stencil flat in a large envelope or file folder.

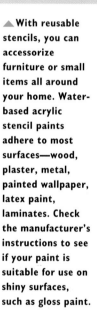

▲ With reusable stencils, you can accessorize furniture or small items all around your home. Water-based acrylic stencil paints adhere to most surfaces—wood, plaster, metal, painted wallpaper, latex paint, laminates. Check the manufacturer's instructions to see if your paint is suitable for use on shiny surfaces, such as gloss paint.

◄ There is no complicated placement or measuring to do— the frog motifs are perfect to stencil randomly, singly or in groups to add a totally individual touch. They make an entertaining decoration for rooms all around the house or even for the patio.

PHOTOGRAPHY BY DAVE KING

PHOTOGRAPHY BY ADRIAN TAYLOR

E·Q·U·I·P·M·E·N·T

YOU WILL NEED:

- Frog stencil (see pages 103-112)
- Water-based stencil paints in green and yellow, with additional colors for details
- Artist's brush
- Scissors
- Household sponge or foam sponge
- Palette or plastic plate for mixing and blending
- Paper towels
- Plain white paper
- Masking tape
- Damp cloth

1 Before you start

- Clean the wall by washing with a warm detergent solution. Rinse and allow to dry.
- Using sharp scissors, cut several 3" x 1" rectangles from the sponge.

2 Paint colors

- Using a palette or plastic plate, pour out a little of each of your chosen stencil paints, mixing some of them together if you want to make your own blended colors. Pour out only a little at a time—water-based stencils paints dry very fast, forming a skin over the surface.

3 Sponge test

- Dab a piece of sponge in the paint to coat the end—try not to pick up too much paint, as a little goes a long way. Dab off any excess paint on a paper towel—this will also eliminate any bubbles. Never start stenciling with too much paint, or it may smudge under the bridges of the stencil.

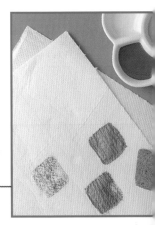

Before you start, make sure you know the effects you will get from blending over both wet and dry paints. If you add a second color over the top of a still-wet paint, you will mix the colors themselves; if you wait until the first paint is dry, you can vary the degree to which the first color shows through the second by adjusting the pressure with which you apply the next layer of paint. If you choose, you can cover up a dry color completely.

5 Stencil test

● Before you start, experiment with blending techniques by using the stencil on white paper. This will help you gauge the amount of paint you need and the different ways of coloring the motifs using varying degrees of pressure.

6 Tape the stencil in place

● Using a damp cloth, wipe the stencil to remove any wet paint and pat it dry with a paper towel. Choose where you want to place your first motif and tape the stencil to the wall, using a piece of masking tape on each side. Do not use ordinary adhesive tape, as this may lift off the background paint when you remove the stencil from the wall.

7 The first color

● With the stencil securely in position on the wall, dip the sponge in the darker of your chosen colors, wipe off the excess and start dabbing paint around the outside edges of the body of the frog, using a light pouncing motion to apply the paint. Build up a little at a time to make the color as solid as you want.

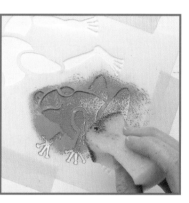

8 Second color

● When the first color has dried, take a different piece of sponge and load it with paint. Dab off the excess as before, then use the same light pouncing motion to fill in the center of the frog. Overlap the existing color lightly in some areas to give a mottled, 3-D effect. Blend the colors by continuing to dab; if you want a darker appearance, only overlap the second color a little. For a much lighter look, keep dabbing to make the second color more dominant on the design.

■ The two frog designs are perfect as single motifs or for repeating patterns or random groups. Clean the stencil thoroughly and flip it over to give variety to the shapes and make the motifs more versatile.

4 Color test

● With just a little paint on the sponge, test the color on a piece of plain white paper, using different degrees of pressure to see the effects.
● When the first color is dry (this takes only a few minutes), use a new piece of sponge to pick up the second color of paint in the same way. Dab next to and over the top of the first color, blending the colors as you continue dabbing.

HELP FILE

SURFACES
When stenciling for the first time, choose a surface that is reasonably flat and smooth, so that the stencil sits flush against the wall with no gaps. To stencil on painted brick, as shown at left, see the Tips on page 96.

SMUDGES
Do not worry if paint smudges under the edges of the stencil. Allow it to dry completely, then touch it up later using a little of the background color, as on page 96.

FILLING IN
If you find you have not sponged color right to the edges of the design when you peel the stencil off, wait until the paint is dry, reposition the stencil exactly over the top of the motif and fill in any blank areas.

SPRAY ADHESIVE
Low-tack, reposition-able adhesive spray is available from arts and crafts suppliers. This spray is less sticky than standard spray adhesive and is ideal for attaching stencils. Use a cloth and a little lighter fluid to clean the back of the stencil after use.

Recreate the charm of a country kitchen with colorful cherry blossom sprigs and richly plumed birds.

Cherry blossom

Blossom-laden boughs and luscious mouth-watering cherries, with bright birds perched among the leaves, bring a breath of fresh country air into any kitchen or dining room. Stenciled in an attractive border or on plain painted furniture, this cherry blossom stencil creates a coordinated American country look. And you can pick out motifs to use separately in your scheme—sprigs of cherries, a scattering of cherry blossoms, a bird or just a single leafy branch.

Stencil in two parts

To create a cherry blossom and bird border, you can use the stencil in two stages—first painting the bough, then adding the bird. Since the bird is stenciled over the bough, you must ensure that no color from the bough bleeds through. The most effective way to do this is to use a template and masking tape, masking off the sections of the bough where the bird overlaps.

PHOTOGRAPHY BY DAVE KING

YOU WILL NEED:
- Cherry blossom stencil, p. 103-112
- Water-based stencil paints in pink, yellow, dark green, light green, red, blue, brown and white
- Stencil brushes
- Fine artist's brush
- Palette
- Scissors
- Masking tape
- Paper towels
- Soft lint-free cloth
- Plastic wrap
- Pencil
- Plain white paper

1 Position the stencil

- Mask off bird motif and tape bough in place. Using the brush, stencil pink and yellow flowers, green leaves and red cherries.

2 Clean the stencil

- When you have finished stenciling the first bough, clean the stencil thoroughly. Lay it paint side up on paper towels or brown kraft paper and wipe clean using the lint-free cloth. Turn it over and wipe again.

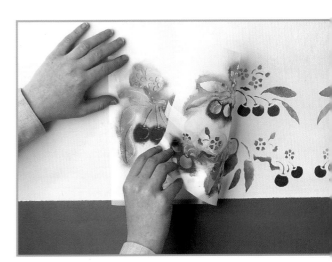

4 Stencil the second bough

● Stencil the second bough, using the same colors as in step 1. Peel away the stencil and then clean it thoroughly.

5 Keep the paint fresh

● To keep the stencil paint fresh while you plan your next few steps, cover the paint palette with plastic wrap.

6 Trace the bird outline

● Peel the masking tape off the bird; using a sharp pencil, trace the outline on a sheet of plain paper. You do not need to trace the detail from the bird's tail; the outline is sufficient.

PAINT BY ARTHUR SANDERSON & SONS LTD. FABRIC BY JANE CHURCHILL FABRICS AND WALLPAPERS

3 Flip the stencil

● Place the stencil so that it runs in the opposite direction to the first set of motifs. Place it by eye—the cherries on each bottom branch [ ] be about ¾" apart. Tape into position.

7 Cut out your template

● Connect the gaps on the traced bird outline and cut around it carefully.

8 Position the bird

● Place the bird template on the stencil so that its feet sit on the lower branch. Its body will cover the top branch.

9 Mark the branch

● Mark the stencil where the bird's body obscures the top branch and its feet cover the bottom branch.

10 Mask off the branch

● Mask off the stencil inside your pencil guidelines. Use small pieces of masking tape, building them up to cover the area.

11 Stencil the branch with gaps

● Place the masked-off branch on the wall, using your second stenciled bough as a guide. Tape into place, stencil and allow paint to dry to the touch.

12 **Place the bird motif**

● Place the bird motif carefully on the branch so that its feet and body fit neatly into the gaps.

■ Before you start stenciling, practice blending colors for the cherry bough and leaves on a scrap of paper. For the cherry leaves and stems, blend two shades of green and add a touch of brown to give a natural effect. Vary the colors to give a lighter or darker effect. Use light and dark brown for the branches—add a touch of white to lighten the brown stencil paint.

■ If you are stenciling a long border, it is a good idea to work out beforehand how many boughs this will take. Starting at the edge of the wall, place the stencil and mark at each end with pencil. Repeat along the wall. At this stage, you can also decide which boughs will have birds. If you are stenciling a border on furniture, it is also best to check first how many motifs will fit so that you can then plan your design accordingly.

■ If your kitchen or dining room does not have a chair rail or natural line for your cherry blossom border to follow, you will have to draw some guidelines. Use a piece of chalk and string as a quick way of marking (see Bramble Border, page 40).

13 **Stencil the bird**

● Tape the bird in place and stencil, blending shades of blue and pink for the body, yellow and red for the legs and head, red for the beak and brown for the eye.

! When you are stenciling your border, don't be tempted to use too many birds, as this will make the branches seem cluttered. A few birds carefully placed will look much better. One bird every third bough should be enough.

14 **Add highlights**

● Using the fine artist's brush and white stencil paint, add highlights to the bird's eye.

15 Peel off stencil

● Peel off the stencil to reveal the bird. You can touch up any faint areas using the fine artist's brush.

16 Add cherry highlights

● Add highlights to the cherries, using white paint and the fine artist's brush. You do not have to highlight every cherry, just one or two on each bough.

Design Ideas

● Pick out separate motifs from the cherry blossom stencil and use them on furniture for a coordinated look. For a fantasy effect, stencil your bird and bough in unusual colors. Gold and black stenciled on a pale background is a striking combination. Or use a single color for the cherries, blossom, bough and bird—red stenciled on white gives a fresh look.

● Stencil a few motifs on fabric for curtains, tie-backs or for seat covers. Use a simple design, picking out a sprig of cherries or a cherry blossom spray.

● Continue the cherry blossom border above a window. Link it with the wall border by stenciling sprigs of cherries down each side of the window. Or stencil some cherries or a bird above a utensil rack or paper towel holder.

● Stencil cherries or birds on decorative ceramic canisters as matching accessories.

Stencil Designs

To cut stencils from the designs on these pages, use one of the following methods:

● Trace the stencil motif you want to use onto tracing paper, or using a photocopier, enlarge or reduce the motif to the desired size. Tape a piece of stencil acetate over the motif and trace the outline, using a fine-tip permanent marker. Place the acetate on a cutting mat and use a craft knife to cut out the design.

● Photocopy or trace the image, place it on a cutting board an place a sheet of glass on top of the image. Secure a piece of stencil acetate on top of the glass with masking tape and use a heated stencil cutting pen to cut out the design, taking care to follow the manufacturer's safety instructions.

**Spring flowers,
page 57**

**Jumping frogs,
page 92**

103

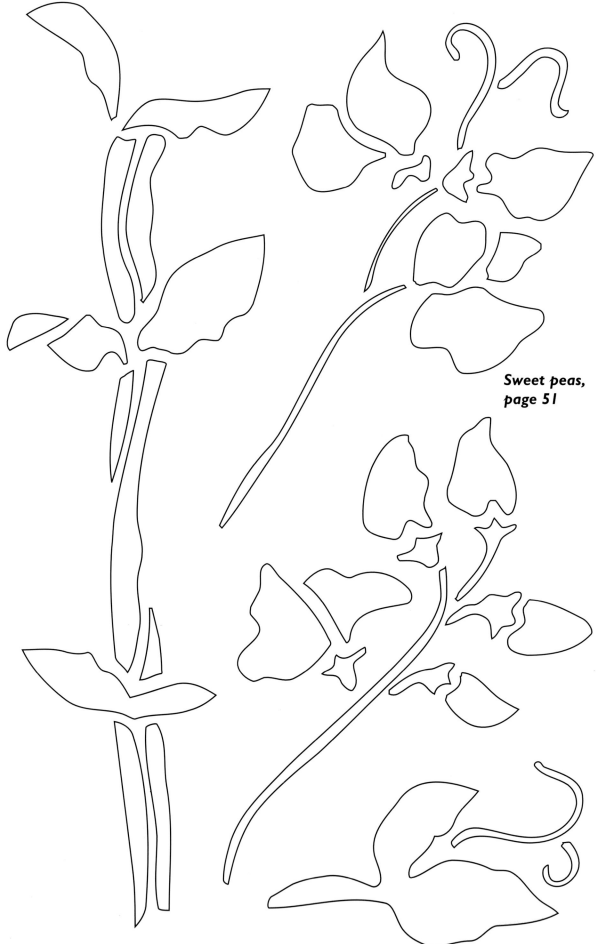

*Sweet peas,
page 51*

Rooster and chicks,
page 73

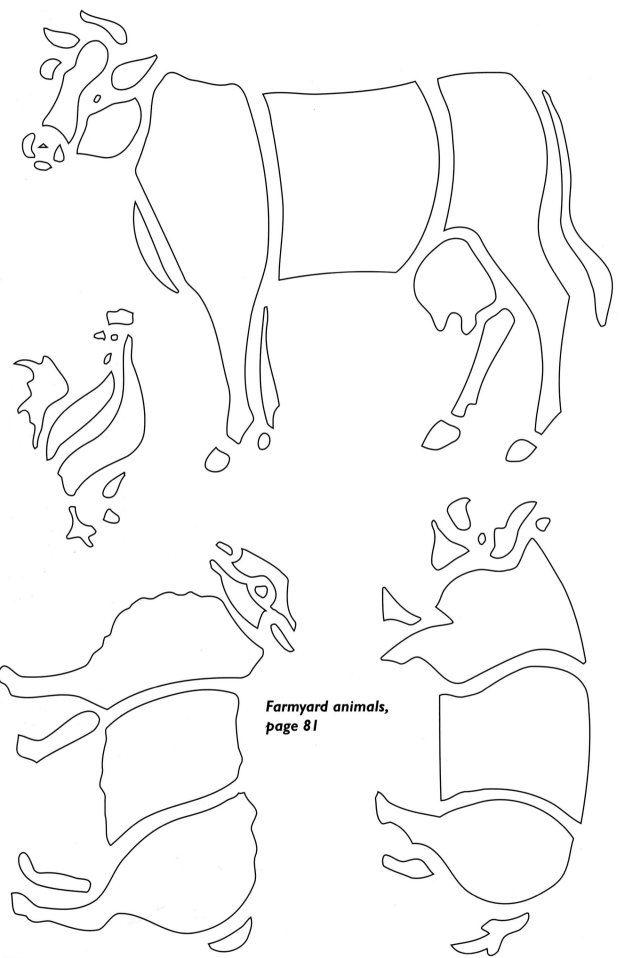

*Farmyard animals,
page 81*

Alphabet, page 86

Wisteria,
page 44

**Bramble Border,
page 38**

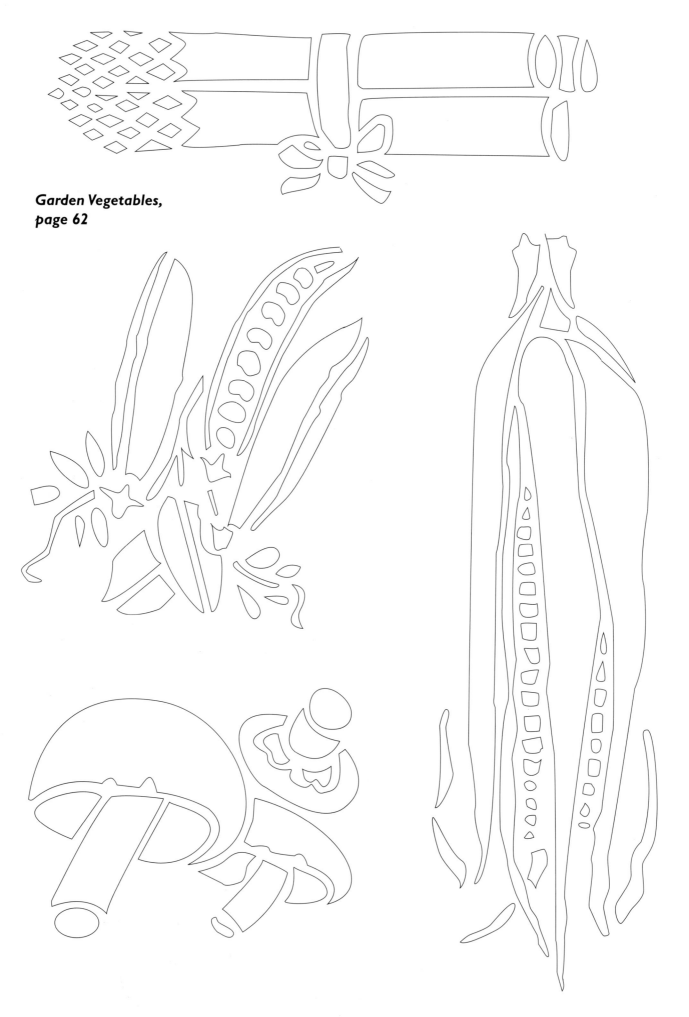

Garden Vegetables,
page 62

Cherry Blossom,
page 97

Willow Pattern,
page 68

CHAPTER 3

Country Techniques

Lumber is expensive, and tongue-and-groove paneling is a major carpentry job—so take the cheaper option with an intriguing paint technique that looks just like the real thing but at a fraction of the cost.

Tongue & groove

YOU WILL NEED:

- 2½ quarts oil-based paint in white
- I quart oil-based paint in dull brown
- 2 quarts oil-based paint in blue-green
- Small quantity of oil-based paint in black (see Materials, right)
- Flat oil-based varnish
- Paint thinner
- Two medium-sized paintbrushes
- Lining brush
- Flat-tipped artist's brush
- Tape measure
- Pencil
- Ruler
- Scissors
- Masking tape
- Two paint pails
- Mixing sticks
- Plumb line
- Mixing bowl

The above quantities are sufficient to "half panel" a 12' x 15' room

Transform any room in the house with a fashionable wainscoting look—or create a Shaker look with three-quarter paneling. You can use any colors you like to fit in with your decorating scheme—the overall effect is of gently aged stained wood.

Although the technique is ideal for walls, try it on laminated furniture, such as plain kitchen cabinets, for a realistic look of wood that is much easier on the eye than solid color. Even if you do not want to create whole walls of the effect, it makes an attractive finish for plain baseboard, which can be given the look of detailed molding with painted lines of light and shadow.

Materials

Start in all cases by giving the walls or furniture a solid coat of white oil-based paint. This forms a base that shows through the finish to give an impression of depth. It is important to use diluted oil-based paint for the grainy layers—this gives a translucent appearance and allows the base to show through. When applying highlight lines, use the lighter of the two diluted colors; for shadows, use either black oil-based paint, as listed at left, or black artist's oil color, diluted with a little paint thinner, to darken the mixture.

Use a lining brush to paint long grain lines—the longer-than-average hairs hold more paint and allow you to paint a longer continuous line before you need to reload the brush. (When you reload your brush, resume painting the line, pressing only lightly, about ¾" before the end of the line, then increase the pressure until the line is the right width.) You can use a soft artist's brush, but you will need to load it with paint more often.

1 Apply the base color

- Draw a horizontal line around the walls at the height you want the paneling. Mask off the area above this line. Pour some brown oil-based paint into a paint pail, dilute with 40% paint thinner and apply below the taped line, using vertical brushstrokes. Press firmly to give a grained look.

2 Remask the paneling

● When the paint is completely dry (this takes about 14 hours), mark at regular intervals 4" down from the top of the painted area; connect these marks using a ruler and pencil. Apply masking tape above this line and if necessary, replace the original top strip of masking tape.

3 Apply a second color

● Dilute some blue-green oil-based paint in a paint pail with 40% paint thinner and paint over the brown graining. Press down as you brush, as before. When dry, remask below the top 4" and apply the paint horizontally to form a "chair rail."

4 Mark panels

● Mark with pencil along the bottom of the "chair rail" at 5¼" intervals. At each mark, using a plumb line, make marks down the wall. Repeat around the room, then connect the vertical marks to define the panels. Mark along the chair rail at ¾", 1½" and 3" depths from the top. Join these horizontal points, using a ruler and pencil.

5 Define the panels

● Load the lining brush with the blue-green paint mixture and paint a line down the left side of every vertical pencil line (see Tips, page 121). All ow to dry completely—this should not take longer than 5 hours.

Don't be tempted to make the diluted paint too thick—to give the right effect, some of the base color needs to show through.

6 Add a shadow

● In a bowl, make a mixture of the diluted blue-green paint and the black paint in a ratio of 4 to 1 respectively. Load the lining brush and paint a line down the right-hand side of every vertical line. Allow to dry for about 5 hours.

7 Trompe l'oeil effect

● Using the fine artist's brush and the black mixture, draw a diagonal line from the top right of the light, defining line, sloping down to a point about ½" lower on the left side of the line. This creates a shadow below the chair rail.

8 Define the chair rail

● Load the lining brush with the blue-green mixture and paint a fairly thick line along the 1½" line, in sections of about 4½' at a time. Using the black mixture paint thinner lines along the ¾" and 3" pencil lines and along the bottom of the chair rail.

9 Soften the lines

● Working quickly before the paint dries, moisten the flat-tipped artist's brush with paint thinner and use it to soften the top and bottom of the 1½" line, breaking it up and creating an impression of depth. Allow to dry.

10 Protect with varnish

● When the paint is completely dry, apply a coat of flat oil-based varnish, working horizontally along the chair rail and downward, as if with the grain of the wood, over the tongue-and-groove paneling.

Color guide

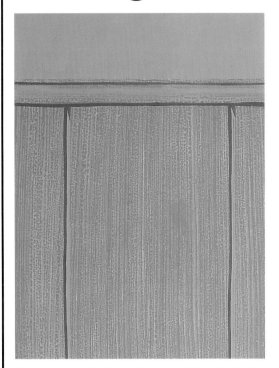

■ Over a base of white paint, apply diluted paint in dark turquoise, then a coat of diluted aqua. Darken the turquoise with black for the shadows and use the aqua for the highlights.

■ Apply a coat of diluted brick red paint over a white background. When dry, add a coat of diluted dull rose. Use the dull rose for highlight lines and darkened red for shadow lines.

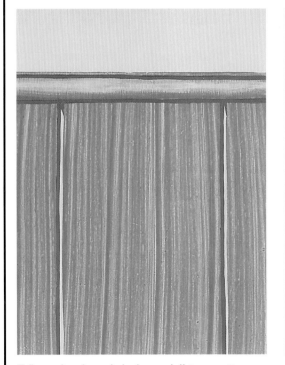

■ For a glazed woody look, use dull terra-cotta over a white background. When dry, add a coat of sandy yellow. If you need to, lighten the yellow paint with a little of the white background paint.

■ For a cool, aquatic look, paint diluted royal blue over a white background and when dry, apply a coat of diluted soft lilac over the top. Dull the royal blue with black for the shadowing.

Although tongue and groove is mainly a technique for walls, try it on smaller items or on plain laminated or painted furniture to create a rustic wood look.

Orange crates

■ Storage boxes are much cheaper to buy if they are made of cardboard rather than wood, and these wood-look "crates" look terrific when painted in wood-stain colors. Start with a coat of primer, then white oil-based paint. When dry, mask off two equal bars across the top of the box and extend these down the sides. Paint these as if with the grain in diluted brown and then, when dry, in a light fawn color. When dry, remask the top and sides of the box to leave only the interlocking panels showing. Repeat the painted graining; when dry, add darkened shadow lines along the edge of each panel and along the angled edges of the box,

Table and chair

■ Coordinate unmatched furniture with this crafty paint effect. Start with a coat of white oil-based paint on the prepared furniture or if the piece is painted in a water-based finish, apply a coat of shellac as a barrier. Paint with diluted Mediterranean blue, then a lighter blue over the top, keeping the brushstrokes in what would be the direction of the grain of the wood. Mark off even wood panels across the width of the table and the chair seat. Add shadows and highlights, as shown in the main technique, and protect with several coats of oil-based varnish.

WOOD-GRAINING

The effect looks like magic but it is so easy to do—in just a few hours you can transform old furniture all around your home with the beautiful knots and grains of natural wood. You do not need to be an expert to follow the simple steps—just use a graining tool to get stunning results.

The art of wood-graining is not new—paint effects experts have copied the elegant natural grains of wood for centuries. There is no mystique to this technique—it is quick and easy to achieve all the effects using one basic tool, and once you start to experiment, the patterns and color combinations are endless.

Wood-graining

Graining tool

A graining tool, with proper care, will last you for years. Always wipe the ridges and teeth of the tool clean between strokes on a rag dipped in paint thinner so as not to blur the graining with glaze from the tool. When you have finished using it, use an old toothbrush or nailbrush and paint thinner to remove every trace of glaze from the ridges and teeth. Wash the tool in warm, soapy water, then rinse and pat dry. Never let glaze dry on the tool and never soak the tool in paint thinner.

Spread out cloths or paper towels that you have used to wipe your graining tool so that they can dry thoroughly with air circulating around them. Throw them away when they are completely dry—oil-based glaze is highly flammable and can catch fire if you leave cloths saturated in it to dry in a confined space.

NADIA MACKENZIE

To produce these eye-catching effects, paint a translucent colored glaze over a plain painted base, then draw a rocker-type graining tool through the glaze. Like magic, it removes the glaze in stripes, leaving the wood-grained pattern. With just three basic strokes of the tool, you can create straight grain, heart grain and large knots; use the comb edge to achieve a plain, fine grain.

Getting started

It is important to work on a completely smooth, nonporous base, so you need to buy your chosen background color in a flat- or satin-finish oil-based paint (gloss paint is too shiny and would repel the glaze). For the second color you need artist's oil color (available in tubes from art supply shops), paint thinner and oil-based glaze, which you can buy at a

home improvement store or paint store.

Our step-by-step instructions show how to transform laminated cabinet doors—but you can apply the technique to any wood-graining job. Wood-graining is fun to do, with wonderful results. Practice your technique with the graining tool to produce effortless and beautiful wood effects to use all around your home.

BEFORE

1 Prepare the surface

Whatever surface you plan to paint needs to be completely clean and free of grease. Wash well with a solution of a mild all-purpose cleaner, then sand with fine-grade

sandpaper so that paint will adhere. Wipe away any dust left by the sanding. This is particularly important when preparing laminated surfaces that would not readily take paint otherwise.

2 Paint the door

Apply paint in your chosen base color to the door. Brush this on thinly, finishing the panel with even vertical strokes, then brushing horizontally across the top and bottom of the frame and vertically down the sides. Two thin coats will give a better surface than one thick one and will dry more quickly. Allow up to 16 hours for the paint to dry between coats.

3 Mix the glaze

Squeeze small blobs of artist's oil color into a saucer and add paint thinner, mixing well. By diluting the color first, you will avoid getting lumps of color in the glaze. Mix the colored paint thinner into the oil-based glaze in a 1-to-1 ratio so that the glaze is like thin cream.

E·Q·U·I·P·M·E·N·T

YOU WILL NEED:
- Graining tool
- 1 quart satin-finish oil-based paint in background color
- Artist's oil colors
- 1 quart oil-based glazing liquid
- 1 quart paint thinner
- 2" paintbrush
- Small brush for glaze
- Short-haired fitch (artist's bristle brush)
- Fine-grade sandpaper
- Paper towels

The above quantities are sufficient to wood-grain the cabinet doors of an average-sized kitchen

PHOTOGRAPHY BY ADRIAN TAYLOR

HELP FILE

EASY TO CORRECT
If you are not happy with the effect when you start graining or find you want to adjust the color, use a cloth dampened with paint thinner and wipe the surface completely clean. You can now start again. When working with glaze over an oil-based background, it is easy to correct mistakes.

COARSE GRAINING
If your graining looks thick with dragged edges, your glaze is probably too thick. Wipe the glaze away with paint thinner, then dilute your glaze with a little more paint thinner. If the weather is very warm, you may find you need to do this several times to keep the glaze workable.

BLURRED PATCHES
This usually comes from applying the glaze too thickly. Use your brush to remove some of the glaze and spread it more thinly, then start again. You get the most subtle effects when some areas of the glaze are thin and the base color shows through, so apply the glaze evenly but thinly.

TOO BUSY
Although knotting and heart-graining are the most eye-catching effects, too much of these grains will look busy if used on the same surface. The overall appearance will be more realistic and look less busy if you alternate between these effects and straight, fine graining done with the comb edge of the graining tool.

Straight grains

● Brush the glazing liquid over the dry base coat, as at left, to cover an area from one side about 6" wide and the full height of the door panel. Apply the glaze thinly so that the base color is just visible, using even vertical brushstrokes in the direction in which you want the grain to run.

● Set the tool down at the very top edge of the glazed area and draw it toward you to the bottom, as in illustration A, below. Apply more glaze so that you work the next stroke on a freshly painted area. Wipe the tool after each stroke.
● For a vein grain, use the comb edge of the tool, drawing it down twice over the same area to give a fine, lined effect.

Heart grain and knots

● Brush glazing liquid over the door, as above. Setting the bottom edge of the tool's curved face down on the top edge of the door, hold the tool at arm's length and draw it

toward you steadily, following the step-by-step illustrations B for heart grain, below. As you do so, gradually rock the tool so that at the end of the stroke you have reached the bottom edge of the door and the top edge of the tool is flat on the door. Wipe the tool clean after each stroke.
● For knotted grain, draw the tool toward you as above, this time rocking it through

several times in one stroke (see illustrations C, below).
● Intersperse heart-grained and knotted stripes with fine vein grain, as shown above. The effect is easier on the eye and looks more natural.

TIPS

PANELED DOOR
On a door with a central panel, grain the center first, then grain across the top and bottom horizontals of the frame. While the worked area is still wet, brush glaze down the vertical sides of the door to overlap the top and bottom horizontals to the width of the side panels, then grain from top to bottom.

A STRAIGHT GRAIN
● For straight graining, hold the tool at arm's length and without rocking it, use your whole arm to draw it straight back toward you through the glaze. Wipe the tool clean after every stroke.

B HEART GRAIN
● Hold the graining tool at arm's length so that the bottom edge is on the glaze at the very top edge of the area to be grained. Draw the tool toward you, gradually rocking the curved face by tipping your wrist, so that you have tilted it through completely by the end of the stroke.

Dealing with panels

To grain the frame around a panel, brush glazing liquid across the top and bottom stiles and grain horizontally from one edge of the door to the other. While this is still wet, brush glaze vertically down the rails, covering the stiles to the width of the panel. Grain from top to bottom on each side.

To fill in the recess around the panel, use a small brush to cover with glazing liquid, then use a dry brush to add texture, working along the grooves.

Golden rules

● Always wipe the ridges of the graining tool clean between strokes, using a cloth dipped in paint thinner.
● Never pause or reposition the graining tool in midstroke.
● Always apply glaze sparingly in the same direction as the graining. Allow at least eight hours to dry.

Finishing touches

● If there are vertical lines of glaze where strokes abut, use a small, dry brush and gently soften lines away, using light vertical strokes.
● For small knots, use a firm fitch and twirl it lightly in the wet glaze, splaying the bristles for a twisted knot.

Softening

● If you want a mellow appearance to your graining, use a large, dry paintbrush and while the glazing liquid is still tacky, soften the effect by brushing very lightly over the top in the direction of the grain.

DETAILING
In wider recessed detailing on a paneled door, use the comb edge of the tool along the length of the recesses. If the top and bottom of the recess curve gently and form part of the panel, grain across them in short vertical strokes with the comb to align with the grain in the panel itself.

c KNOTTED GRAIN
● Hold the tool at arm's length and as you draw it toward you, rock it through as for heart grain but this time rock it back and forth two or three times during the stroke, as below.

Before

Chest of drawers

To transform a laminated chest of drawers, wood-grain in deep brown over mahogany red. Prepare the surface as on page 111, then follow the steps on pages 112-113 and below for a professional finish.

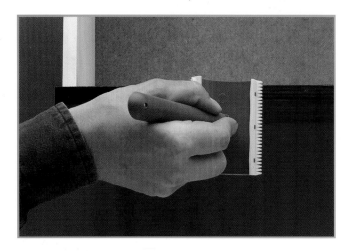

1 To grain the thin top edges of the drawers, brush on the glaze, then use one edge of the graining tool, holding it steady, as for straight graining. Draw the tool along the length of the drawer to give a straight grain with no knots.

2 For a professional finish, use a large, dry paintbrush to soften the graining effect. Using only the very tips of the bristles, brush very gently over the still slightly wet glaze. This will not smudge the graining but will give it a softer appearance.

● This soft, sage green graining is very simple but effective. We used a ready-mixed glaze, available from some craft shops, over a base of white paint.

● This soft wood-graining is done with a glaze of Payne's gray over a pale blue background. Color combinations do not have to be realistic to look good.

Fantasy colors

Experiment with colors—you can copy natural effects or create fabulous blends or contrasting combinations.

● Paint the base with a soft, sandy yellow, then mix the glaze with raw sienna oil color to produce a sunny finish that is just a little brighter than natural pine.

● The base color for this combination was white oil-based paint, and the wood-graining over it is in very pale yellow to give a soft and gentle contrast.

● This dazzling, fiery look comes from graining in viridian-colored glaze over a background of orange—a truly fantastic and adventurous finish.

Pigment
PAINTING

Use the rich, powdery colors of paint pigments to create textured finishes and masked-off designs with a fresh and rustic look.

Powder pigments are what give the basic coloring for paint—from school art-class paints to fine art colors. The quality of these varies from inexpensive economy-sized jars of coarse powder to the dustlike pigments favored by artists. For working on large areas, such as a wall, these cheap-and-cheerful powders, available in art supply stores, are ideal—they are bright, easy to use and go a long way.

The coarse texture of these pigments makes them ideal for creating brushy, rustic textures. And unless you blend them before applying, the effect of having two colors on your brush can be quite spectacular, with streaks of pure color standing out on a blended background.

Powder paint

These dry pigments need to be applied in a medium that will make them stick to the surface. The surface can be sealed with varnish for a finish that will not flake off.

EQUIPMENT

YOU WILL NEED:
- Powder pigments in gold, bronze, yellow, red, white and blue
- Ready-mixed wallpaper paste
- Spray varnish
- Four medium-sized paintbrushes
- Household sponge
- Two small paintbrushes
- Tape measure
- Chalk
- Set square

- Ruler
- Scissors
- Masking tape in ½", ¾" and 1" widths
- Brown paper or scrap paper
- Two drop cloths
- Eight mixing bowls
- Mixing sticks
- Plastic cups
- Pen
- Plain white paper
- Stencil acetate
- Cutting mat or board
- Craft knife
- Low-tack spray adhesive
- Cloth

2 Mask off design

● Mask off the outside of the design with 1"-wide masking tape, using brown paper to protect the wall around the outer rectangle. Run ¾"-wide tape along the center of the remaining chalk lines. Use a drop cloth to protect the floor.

3 Add details

● Draw lines in chalk to divide the center rectangle into 3 equal horizontal bands. Run ½"-wide tape along the center of the horizontal lines. Divide the outside border into 4" squares, using a ruler and chalk.

1 Measure the design

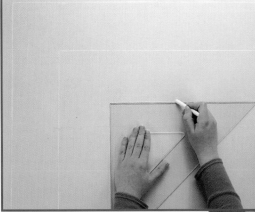

● Draw chalk lines 6 ½" and 38½" up from the floor. Using the set square, connect the lines to make a 68"-long rectangle. Draw 2 more rectangles that are 4½" and 9 ¼" respectively in from the outside edge of the largest rectangle.

4 Pick up paste and powder

● Mix a little gold, bronze and yellow pigment in a bowl; pour some wallpaper paste into a plastic cup. Over brown paper, load a medium-sized brush with paste, wiping off excess against the side of the cup. Dip the brush in the pigment, shaking off loose powder.

6 Paint pink border

● Mask off the gold border with a drop cloth. Mix red and yellow pigment; load a dry brush as in step 4 and paint the middle border, working in strokes along and around the frame shape.

7 Brush white over pink

● Load a dry medium-sized brush with white pigment and when the pink border is dry to the touch, brush on the pigment using short, random strokes, blending the white into the pink to create a cloudy texture. Reload the brush with white when necessary, then allow to dry.

■ Use the design on the left to cut a simple stencil or use a motif from the patterns from pages 103-112 or one taken from an element of your existing decor.

5 Paint the border

● Paint each square of the outer border, alternating the direction of the brushstrokes between vertical and horizontal on adjacent squares to give a checkered effect. Reload the brush with paste and powder as necessary. Allow to dry completely, about 2-4 hours.

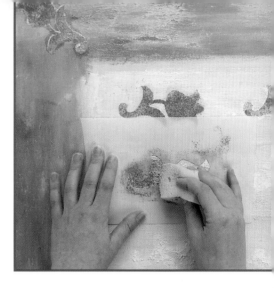

8 Paint yellow bands

● Reposition the drop cloth to cover the pink border. In a bowl, mix yellow and white pigment and paint the remaining areas, loading the brush with paste and pigment as before. When this is dry to the touch, brush on some dry white pigment. Remove the drop cloth and allow paint to dry for at least 4 hours.

9 Cut a stencil

● Trace the tulip design from page 131 on a sheet of white paper. Place the stencil acetate on top of the tracing, securing both to a cutting mat with masking tape. Using a craft knife, cut a stencil by following the outline of the tracing.

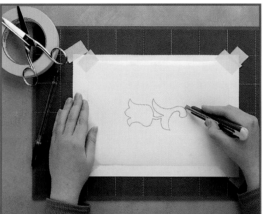

10 Mix powder and paste

● In a bowl, mix a little white pigment with some wallpaper paste, stirring well until the color is evenly distributed. If the mixture is very stiff, add a little water until the consistency is more manageable.

11 Stencil the motif in white

● Place the stencil at the corner of the pink border and using a sponge, stencil with the white paste mixture. Repeat at the other corners of the pink border, then stencil along the horizontal strips, leaving a gap of approximately 1½" between the motifs. Allow to dry for 2 hours.

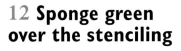

12 Sponge green over the stenciling

● In a bowl, mix blue and yellow pigment to make green. Reposition the stencil over the white motif and with a clean, slightly damp sponge, stencil each motif in green. Allow to dry for 2 hours.

■ The charm of pigment paints is their grainy texture and uneven cover. This alcove has been decorated to contrast sharply with the solid, matte-painted walls around it—not only in its colors but in its textures too.

The sparse cover of vertical brushstrokes allows the background color to show through in some areas, such as near the top shelf where traces of yellow are visible. You can also add texturing in a lighter color to give a more broken effect— white dry-brushed over the almost-dry blue pigment softens the effect of an otherwise very powerful color.

Coarse pigment paints are not designed for fine work, so avoid intricate freehand designs. Instead, stick to bold panels of color and patterns that can be created using masking tape or simple stencils.

It is important to seal the finish with varnish to prevent any surface powder from wearing off. Because the action of brushing from one color area to another is likely to smudge the pigments, use a spray varnish and apply it lightly to avoid drips and dribbles.

13 Paint blue border

● Remove all the tape except that around the outside of the design and mask off the newly painted areas. In a bowl, mix blue pigment with some wallpaper paste, as in step 10. Using a small brush, paint a solid coat of blue inside the masked-off center areas.

14 Brush on blue pigment

● When the blue is dry to the touch, load a small brush with dry blue pigment. Gently brush over the blue, blending the dry pigment into the finish. Allow to dry for 2 hours, before removing the tape applied in step 13.

! This technique can be messy—remove any furnishings from the room and cover the floor with drop cloths, securing them firmly to the baseboards. Dry pigment will float in the air, so keep the room well-ventilated while you are working.

TIPS

■ When brushing on dry pigment, the brush needs to be absolutely dry. Keep one brush separate for this job, using a damp cloth to wipe away any pigment left when you have finished using a color.

■ You can use a hairdryer to speed up the drying times, but set it on a low heat and hold it at a distance of about 12" to prevent the paint finish from cracking.

■ Instead of buying spray varnish, pour some water-based varnish into a spray bottle, diluting it with water if its consistency is too thick.

■ Do not attempt to apply the pigment-colored paste over shiny surfaces, such as gloss or satin-finish paints, as it will not adhere long enough to dry in place.

■ Use the set square to check that the angles of the rectangles in the border are perfect right angles.

■ Cut the stencil acetate to fit the horizontal strips, leaving 1½" of acetate to the left of the design. Also cut the bottom of the acetate to line up with the bottom edge of the horizontal strip.

15 Distress with white

● Load a medium-sized brush with dry white pigment and apply it in random patches over the design. Blend the color into the finish to create a soft, distressed look. Allow to dry for at least 2 hours.

! When you apply the varnish, it will darken the pigment colors by several tones. Test the colors on scrap paper before starting a project to make sure you get the final effect you want.

16 Spray varnish

● If the surface is likely to suffer a lot of wear and tear, spray with an even coat of varnish to darken the color to its final tone. Once dry, remove all the masking tape, brown paper and drop cloths.

Color guide

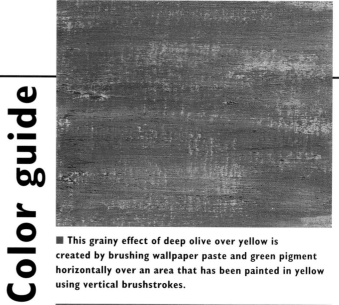

■ This grainy effect of deep olive over yellow is created by brushing wallpaper paste and green pigment horizontally over an area that has been painted in yellow using vertical brushstrokes.

■ Because you can apply pigment colors as heavily or as lightly as you like, they are ideal for shading. This sunset effect is a graduated brushing of red pigment and wallpaper paste over a base of yellow flat latex paint.

■ Experiment with simple colors and textures—the wallpaper-paste-and-pigment mixture takes up to four hours to dry, so you can scratch away the surface layer of pigment to leave an etched pattern where the base color shows through. If you make a mistake or are not happy with the effect, simply brush on more paste and pigment and start again.

If you want to create a particularly coarse, powdery finish, use a dry brush to stroke on extra dry pigment, working it gradually into the background of pasted color, then seal it with at least one coat of spray varnish.

Aged TERRA-COTTA

Give plain pottery **or crockery a** rustic look **with this simple but effective** coloring and texturing **technique.**

Take advantage of the versatile properties of red oxide metal primer. Not only is it an ideal color for terra-cotta effects, it is also a durable undercoat for all sorts of surfaces—metals, plastic, pottery, china—enabling you to convert a set of old metal carryalls into rustic containers or coordinate tired-looking vases with a new and fashionable finish.

Materials

Two sponges make ideal and inexpensive "tools" to adapt for this technique. You can create a loose texture like natural sponge on one and use the torn texture of a second to give a heavier covering of paint.

Red oxide metal primer will adhere to most surfaces, but if your pot, vase or carryall is very shiny or has a very smooth, glazed finish, sand the item lightly all over with fine-grade sandpaper so that the paint will adhere.

It is important to let each layer of paint dry completely before adding the next—remember that this primer will need about 24 hours to be dry enough to work on.

PHOTOGRAPHY BY LIZZIE ORME

YOU WILL NEED:
- Red oxide metal primer
- Small amount of flat latex paint in terra-cotta and blue-gray
- Spray paint in cream
- Wood stain in walnut
- Paint thinner
- Medium-sized paintbrush
- Two household sponges
- Scissors
- Plastic drop cloth
- Plastic plates

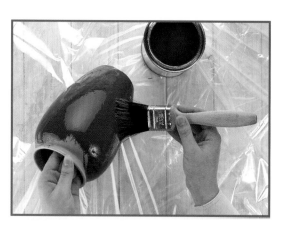

1 Apply the base coat

Make sure the surface of the piece you are going to paint is completely grease-free and dry. Working over the drop cloth, apply an even coat of red oxide paint.

2 Stipple the paint

After about 5 minutes, when the paint has become slightly tacky, stipple the surface using the tip of the paintbrush to give a slightly textured finish. Allow to dry for about 24 hours.

4 Sponging on terra-cotta

● Pour a little of the terra-cotta paint on a plastic plate; still working on the drop cloth, use the textured sponge to dab thick, uneven patches of color over the red paint. Take care to let the base show through in patches.

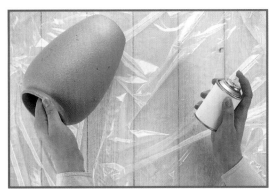

5 Spray with cream paint

● Wait until the sponged terra-cotta is completely dry, then spray liberally and unevenly with cream spray paint, keeping the pot on the drop cloth to protect your work surface. Allow to dry—this will take about 1 hour.

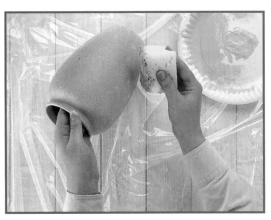

6 Sponging on blue-gray

● Pour a little of the blue-gray paint on a plastic plate; use the torn edge of one-half of the second sponge to apply color in random patches all over the pot, letting the base colors show through. Allow to dry for 2–4 hours.

3 Prepare the sponges

● Using the scissors to round off the corners and snip, and your thumb and forefinger to pinch, texture a sponge so that it is like a natural one. Tear a second sponge in half.

TIPS

■ Red oxide metal primer makes a durable undercoat for all sorts of painted finishes but it is impossible to remove from clothes or carpets. Always work over a drop cloth or newspaper.

■ In place of cream spray paint, use a stencil brush with either cream latex paint or acrylic stencil paint. Pick up a small amount of paint on the brush and stipple randomly over the surface.

■ If you find that you have obliterated too much of any color with the subsequent layer of paint, simply sponge on a little more until you get the effect you want.

■ When using spray paint, follow the manufacturer's instructions and work in a well-ventilated room. For prolonged use, wear a protective mask to avoid inhaling droplets in the air.

■ If you have trouble getting the red oxide inside the lip of a pot or vase, either use a radiator brush with an angled handle or apply the paint with a small wedge of sponge, wearing protective gloves to keep the metal primer off your hands.

7 Sponging on terra-cotta

● Using the second half of the torn sponge, dip the torn surface in the terra-cotta paint on the plate and dab it unevenly over the dry surface of the pot. Allow to dry for 2–4 hours.

7 Finish with wood stain

● Apply an even coat of walnut wood stain over the whole pot, working over the lip beyond where the finish is visible. Allow to dry completely—about 1 hour.

Design ideas

Using a base of red oxide metal primer, you can vary the tone of the sponged colors over the top to create different effects. Try a dull blue-green as the second sponged color and experiment with different colors of wood stain as the finishing coat.

If you want to raise a more pronounced texture on the surface, sprinkle a little sand randomly over the red oxide while it is still tacky (be sparing, or the effect will be coarse and clumsy). Complete the technique in the same way.

The effect looks just as convincing on flowerpots, planters or jardinieres that have a relief pattern. The sponging will tend to be strongest on the areas that stand out the most, creating a realistic aged effect. If you want to work the sponged colors into the details of the pattern, use a stencil brush loaded with a small amount of paint to stipple lightly into the crevices.

Crackle-finish cabinet

Add a touch of aged style to the plainest accessories with this simple two-layer varnish technique. You need no special skills to transform a new pine wall cabinet into an "antique" heirloom in next to no time—the crackle medium does the work for you.

rackle painting is an increasingly popular way to add character and age to new furniture and accessories. It is the easiest of all aging techniques—and you can achieve stunning effects simply by using two different types of varnish.

Start with a plain base coat and brush on an oil-based varnish. When this is nearly dry, brush on a coat of water-based varnish—and before your eyes, random cracks will start to appear.

This technique is very versatile; you get different looks with different types of varnish or different colors of paint. For a traditional, rich "antique" effect, varnish the original surface with the two coats as described in the steps on the right, then rub in some artist's oil color to highlight the cracks. A base of strong red, green or yellow is particularly effective treated in this way. Or, if you use pastel colors as a base and then rub in some gilt paste, the cracks will have a golden color. You can make the effect as soft or as dramatic as you like.

Suitable surfaces

Boxes, picture frames, wooden candlesticks and flea-market finds are all ideal subjects for crackle painting, and it is a technique suitable for most surfaces—metals, woods, even plastics—as long as you prime the surface appropriately. Whatever primer you use, always follow the manufacturer's instructions and make sure the area you want to treat is clean and unwaxed (see Help File for advice and suggestions on what primers to use).

Complete crackle-finish kits are available in crafts shops and paint stores and by mail order. The kits are designed to give very quick results, with all you need in one pack. However, you can get just the same results with the materials listed—you will be surprised how easy it is.

PHOTOGRAPHY BY STEVE DALTON

EQUIPMENT

YOU WILL NEED:
- Artist's oil color in mid-green and burnt umber
- Small can oil-based varnish
- Small can water-based varnish (or crackle-finish kit)
- Two ½" paintbrushes
- Fine-grade sandpaper
- Household sponge
- White glue and glue brush
- Lint-free cloths
- Plastic plate or palette
- Scissors
- Picture cut from magazine or gift wrap
- Ruler

1 Preparation

● The cabinet shown here is made from varnished pine; it is essential that you prepare your piece thoroughly before decorating. Remove the wooden knob from the door and set aside. Rub down any existing varnish, using fine-grade sandpaper; wipe with a clean, damp cloth so that the surface is completely free from dust. If you are working on bare wood, treat any knots with a shellac-based sealer to prevent resin from seeping through and marking the finish.

2 Applying the base coat

● Squeeze a dab of green artist's oil color onto a plastic plate. Using a small piece cut from the sponge, apply the paint to the cabinet, working in the direction of the grain and rubbing the paint in evenly. Work around all sides of the door, wiping off excess paint from hinges. We used a mid-green color, but any strong shade would be as effective for an antique look. Use a pastel color for a softer and more subtle effect. Allow to dry completely.
● If you wish to use a wood wash or a water-based paint, apply these with a brush, using even strokes in the direction of the grain, and allow to dry completely.

3 Adding the motif

● Adding a paper motif completely transforms this plain cabinet—but choose your motif so that it looks appropriate to the style you are creating and is in proportion to the finished item (see Help File, right, for ideas). Trim the motif to the size of the door panel. Apply white glue to the door panel and carefully place the motif in the center. Gently press with your fingers, working out from the center toward the sides to ensure there are no air bubbles trapped beneath the surface. Allow the glue to dry completely.

HELP FILE

■ You can use almost any design, picture or motif to decorate the cabinet. A repeat pattern would be ideal for making a border, for example, and cuttings taken from magazines, postcards, photographs or wallpaper would make good centerpieces. Either cut out the pieces individually or cut them to fit the center panel of the cabinet exactly.

■ Since a crackle finish is meant to give an aged effect, Victorian pictures are very appropriate as cuttings. Nature motifs such as shells, flowers or butterflies are pretty, and old photos, especially black and white ones, look very effective.

■ The knots in new wood start to exude a sticky amber-colored resin after a while, and if not treated, this will seep through the base color of your cabinet and stain the surface. To prevent this, brush over the knots with a shellac-based sealer, available at hardware stores and paint stores.

■ To prime new wood for painting, apply a coat of oil- or water-based primer. If you use artist's oil color as a stain, you can apply it directly to untreated wood.

4 Oil-based varnish

● Using a paintbrush, coat the entire cabinet with a thin, even layer of oil-based varnish. For even, straight cracks, apply the varnish in the direction of the grain of the wood. If you feel the varnish is uneven, dampen a cloth with paint thinner and wipe off. Start again when dry. If you feel unsure about tackling a complete object at once, practice on a rough piece of board.
● Clean your brush using paint thinner, then a mild detergent. Rinse until the brush is completely clean.

5 Water-based varnish

● Before the varnish dries completely and while it is still slightly tacky to the touch—this takes about 15–20 minutes—take a fresh paintbrush and apply a generous coating of water-based varnish in the opposite direction to the first coat. The crackle effect starts almost immediately, so try to keep the brushstrokes quick and even, covering each area of the cabinet once only. Allow to dry in a well-ventilated room for several hours or overnight.

6 Giving an antique touch

● To give the crackle finish a genuine "antique" look, darken the cracks using artist's oil in burnt umber to accentuate them. Dab a little from the tube on a lint-free cloth and gently rub over the surface with your fingertips. Allow to almost dry, then rub any excess color off the surface, working inward toward the cracks. Buff with a clean cloth. Paint the existing wooden knob to match the background color, varnish and reattach, or replace it with a brass or china knob that suits the new look. Finish with a coat of clear varnish to shield the surface from damage.

Desk organizer

A plain desktop organizer gets a new lease on life with the crackle-finish treatment. In a few simple steps, it is transformed from a basic but functional container to an elegant, pretty accessory. ▼

TIPS

■ If you want to create deep cracks in the glaze, speed up the drying process by using the warm setting on a hair dryer. Keep moving the dryer evenly over the surface until the varnish is completely dry.

in a steady circular movement. Buff, using a clean cloth, until the surface is clean and the cabinet has a soft shine.

■ When applying the first coat of varnish, try to keep your work surface flat, otherwise the varnish may drip down the sides of the cabinet and cause runs, which would result in larger cracks appearing where the drips run.

■ Use brown shoe polish in place of burnt umber artist's oil color to simulate the darkening of an expensive piece of antique furniture. If you are going to do this, omit step 6, above. Dab a little polish on a clean cloth, then rub the cloth firmly over the surface

■ If you apply the first coat of varnish unevenly and in circular strokes, the resulting cracks will also form uneven patches in circular and swirly shapes. This gives an unusual and interesting effect as a change from the straight crackling.

Bark effect

Inspired by the rough textures and rich colors of untreated wood, this simple faux effect uses paper, acrylic paint and artist's oil colors to capture the broken, weather-beaten look of bark.

Transform a set of book covers with an unusual grainy bark effect. It's an ideal finish to give a soft, informal look to shiny surfaces such as laminates and to add aged charm and character to mass-produced blank covers.

The technique

There is no need to sand the surface you are going to paint as the effect is meant to be uneven. However, if the surface is shiny, it is best to sand it lightly and coat with primer so that the papier-mâché will adhere well.

Perform your face-lift in easy stages. In the first stage, lay down a rough layer of papier-mâché, then when this is dry, add texture and color by breaking up the surface, painting and rubbing with oil color.

The basic technique is the same for effects as diverse as silver birch bark and trees such as beech or sycamore—just use oil colors to suit the look you want to achieve.

Materials

You do not need any special equipment—but it is important that you use a combination of water-based acrylic paint and oil-based colors. (An oil-based paint would not absorb the color as the water-based variety does and it would create too smooth a finish.)

The ideal tool for scoring and texturing the paint is an awl—the short point (normally used for boring holes) makes it easy to control, but you could substitute a short screwdriver if necessary.

1 Tear paper into strips

● Tear the construction paper into random-sized, roughly rectangular strips, making sure that all edges are ragged. Tear up enough paper to cover the surface of your item at least twice.

2 Layer the paper

● Place the item on a drop cloth, then brush the surface liberally with wallpaper paste. Layer the paper on top in overlapping vertical strips, using a generous amount of paste as you add the second layer. Leave any buckles as this adds to the texture. Leave for 6–8 hours until touch-dry.

YOU WILL NEED:
● **Sheets of construction paper or scrap paper** (See Tips for alternate papers that you can use.)
● **Heavy-duty wallpaper paste**
● **Water-based acrylic satin paint in white**

● **Artist's oil color in black, white and burnt umber**
● **Oil-based flat varnish**
● **Paint thinner**
● **Two paintbrushes**
● **Small paintbrush or craft stick (for mixing)**
● **Plastic drop cloth**
● **Awl**
● **Craft knife**
● **Mixing bowl**
● **Tightly-woven cloth (for applying oil color)**

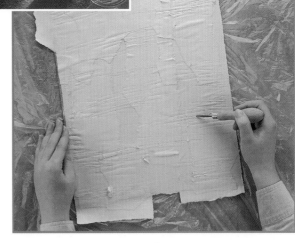

3 Score the paper

● Use an awl to score several roughly parallel horizontal lines across the surface in any areas where it is smooth. Use a craft knife to trim away any excess paper from around the edges of the item. Allow to dry about 1 hour more.

4 Apply the acrylic paint

● When the surface is dry, brush on a thin, uneven coat of white acrylic paint. Do not smooth the paint to neaten the brushstrokes—the random streaky effect is part of the bark texture. Let dry slightly.

5 Scrape off some acrylic

● For this stage, the paint needs to be quite wet. Use a dry paintbrush to scrape across the surface to remove some of the acrylic paint, creating pits and scratches that imitate the rough, broken texture of bark. Let dry for 4 hours.

6 Mix oil colors

● Place a little black and white artist's oil colors in a small bowl and add a tiny amount of burnt umber. Mix with a brush or craft stick to make a pale mid-gray color, stirring well until the color is evenly blended.

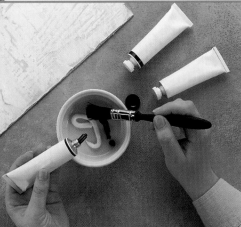

! Make sure the papier-mâché layer is dry enough at step 3 to score without tearing. Similarly, the water-based acrylic paint needs to be completely dry before you start rubbing in the oil color, otherwise it will lift off the surface and you will have to start again.

7 Rub on oil color

● Wrap the cloth around your forefinger and pick up a little oil color. Rub this over the surface, taking care to cover all the scores, scratches and pits. Work over the whole surface, then let dry for 30 minutes.

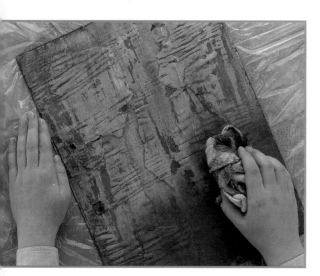

8 Rub back the color

● Use a clean section of the cloth to rub back the oil color, removing some areas more than others, but leaving plenty of oil color in the pitted areas. Allow to dry completely—this will take 12–24 hours.

9 Varnish

● When the surface is completely dry, brush on at least one even coat of oil-based flat varnish, working the brushstrokes in one direction. Allow to dry for 12 hours or according to the manufacturer's instructions.

Oak bark effect

Because bark occurs in many textures and colors, you can adapt this technique to imitate other woods, such as the aged oak effect on the chair, right. The only difference is in the colors of artist's oils to give the right effect.

For oak bark, tear paper into rough ovals of varying sizes and glue them down so that a small one lies over a larger one. When dry, coat with white water-based acrylic paint and scrape back after 30 minutes. Rub burnt umber oil color over the surface when the acrylic is dry. For the textured grain, drag a graining tool straight through the oil color without rocking.

Paint the legs and edges with white acrylic, scraping off areas as before, then rub on some oil color. When dry, coat chair with flat varnish.

Increase your repertoire of faux wood effects with three simple techniques for teak, pine and oak, using a graining tool, flat latex paint and wood stain.

Wood effects

Instead of using a tinted oil-based glaze for wood-graining, explore the potential of using ordinary flat latex paint with the rich, translucent color of wood stain over top. To create the pattern as shown on the door (right), mark out the design as detailed on page 153, then mask off area by area to grain the frame and the upper and right triangles of the center motif as pine, the panels as oak and the rest as teak. Follow the steps for each technique, masking as needed. When the wood effects are dry, outline with a silver permanent marker.

The techniques are deceptively simple, and you need only one piece of special equipment. For the oak effect, you need a rocker-type graining tool, available from craft shops, paint stores and by mail order. Experiment using the oak-graining edge with its angled teeth—by altering the angle you can vary the width of the grain as you work.

Teak effect for molding

Use a simple dry-brushing technique to imitate the flecked grain and rich colors of teak.

EQUIPMENT

YOU WILL NEED:
- Flat latex paint in white
- Water-based wood stain in teak
- Clear water-based varnish

- Large paintbrush
- Two small paintbrushes
- Masking tape
- Flexible masking tape (for curved edges)
- Pencil
- Ruler
- Tape measure
- String
- Scissors
- Pushpin

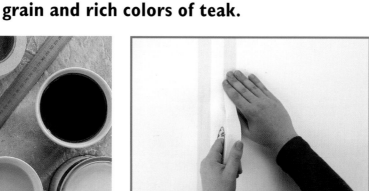

2 Measure the design

● Using the pencil, ruler, tape measure and string, measure and mark the design on the door (see page 153). Once finished, mask around the outside of the molding.

1 Apply the base coat

● Remove any door hardware. With the door lying horizontally, paint the area to be given a teak finish with an even coat of white flat latex paint. Allow to dry for 2-4 hours.

3 Apply the wood stain

● Apply a liberal coat of teak wood stain on the masked-off area, working the brushstrokes in a vertical direction. Allow to dry for at least 2 hours.

PHOTOGRAPHY BY LIZZIE ORME

4 Dry-brush with white

● Load a small paintbrush very sparingly with white latex paint and rub the paint lightly over the wood-stained area so that you leave only a very light covering on the surface and some of the wood stain is still visible. Allow to dry for 2 hours.

5 Apply wood stain

● With a small paintbrush, apply an even coat of teak wood stain over the masked-off area, making sure you cover the white latex paint. Allow to dry for 2–4 hours.

6 Varnish

● Apply a coat of clear water-based varnish. If the item is to be finished with other wood effects, wait until you before you varnish it.

Pine

Use a graining tool and wood stain to create a realistic pine finish.

• E Q U I P M E N T •

YOU WILL NEED:
- ● Flat latex paint in white
- ● Water-based wood stain in antique pine
- ● Clear water-based varnish
- ● Two paintbrushes
- ● Graining tool

1 Brush on wood stain

● Apply an even coat of white latex paint; when dry, mask off the area to be given the pine finish. Apply a liberal coat of antique pine wood stain, working brushstrokes in one direction. Allow to dry for 2–4 hours.

2 Apply white

● Brush on white latex paint in a vertical strip approximately the width of the wood-graining tool.

3 Wood-grain with white

● While the white latex paint is still wet, grain vertically, adding occasional knots (see Wood-graining, pages 121-127). Repeat steps 2 and 3 to grain the whole area. Allow to dry for 2–4 hours.

4 Apply more wood stain

● Apply a second coat of antique pine wood stain, making sure you cover the white latex evenly. Allow to dry for 2–4 hours before varnishing.

Oak

The oak-graining edge of a graining comb creates a wide, straight grain.

YOU WILL NEED:
- Flat latex paint in white
- Water-based wood stain in dark oak
- Clear water-based varnish
- Two paintbrushes
- Graining comb

TIPS

■ To give the wood effect a slightly aged appearance, use antique white flat latex paint instead of brilliant white. For a richer look, mix a little yellow ocher artist's acrylic color into the latex paint for the base coat.

■ The white latex tends to "bleach" the color of the wood stain, so use stain in a color that is at least one tone darker than the effect you wish to achieve.

■ If the white latex becomes too dry to grain before you work on it, wait until it is completely dry, then apply more wood stain to that area. When dry, repaint with latex and grain immediately.

■ Use a tinted varnish for extra depth and to bring an aged look to the wood effect.

■ Always prepare your item properly by sanding the surface so that the base coat will adhere, using an appropriate primer if necessary. When applying the primer and base coat, work the brushstrokes in a vertical direction— that is, in the direction of the grain of the wood.

1 Apply the wood stain

● On a base of dry white latex paint, mask off the area to be oak-grained and apply the dark oak wood stain liberally, working the brushstrokes in one direction. Allow to dry for 2–4 hours.

2 Using the oak grainer

● Apply white latex to an area approximately the width of the graining comb and while it is still wet, draw the oak-graining edge of the comb down toward you, as if it were a haircomb.

3 Combing

● While the paint is still wet, comb over the grained section twice using the narrow-toothed comb edge of the graining comb. Wobble the comb slightly to give a random, wavy look to the combing. Repeat steps 2 and 3 until you have grained the whole area. Allow to dry for 2–4 hours.

4 Apply wood stain

● Apply an even coat of dark oak wood stain over the oak area. Allow t[o] dry for 2–4 hours before varnishing.

Design ideas

■ For a wood-effect tray, start with a base of white latex paint. When dry, top with a layer each of teak and walnut stain, drying between applications. Brush again with the white latex and while still wet, comb through with first straight, then wavy lines, using the fine comb edge of the graining tool. When dry, apply another coat of teak stain. When dry, apply walnut stain; then, when totally dry, protect with a coat of varnish for a durable finish.

■ To give a flea-market bread box a rich antique oak finish, start with a base of white latex paint. When dry, brush with teak stain to give a good depth of color; then, when dry, brush with antique oak stain. Apply white latex over the dry stain and grain horizontally with the rocker face of the graining tool. Comb over the top with the fine comb edge and allow to dry. Apply two coats of antique oak stain, drying between coats, then varnish as above.

■ This platter, used as a cheese board, also started with a base of white latex. The deep color of the base comes from two coats of walnut, and the grain is created by dry-brushing. Pick up a small amount of white latex on a medium-sized paintbrush, wipe off the excess and brush across the platter, keeping the strokes in the same direction; allow to dry. Apply two coats of walnut stain, letting each coat dry, then finish with a coat of varnish. This dry-brushing technique is ideal where a concave edge or surface makes it impossible to use a comb or graining tool.

As you mask off the different areas of the door to give them different wood finishes, make sure that the last area you decorated is completely dry before repositioning the masking tape. Similarly, make sure that the whole surface is completely dry before ruling in the lines around the panels and border with a silver permanent marking pen.

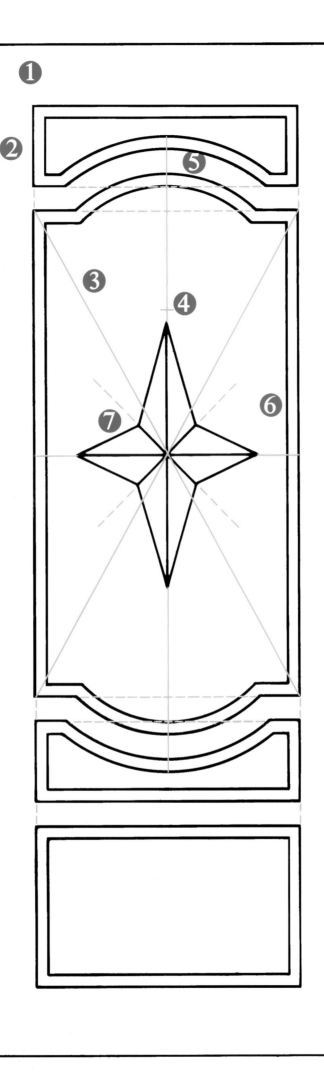

To plan the design

1 Measure a 5" border in from the edge of the door.

2 Measure the height of the center area, subtract 6" from this and divide the remainder by 10. Measure and mark the resulting distance (Y") from the top of the panel. Leave a gap of 2", mark and then measure 6 x Y" from this point for the large panel. Leave a 2" space, then mark another panel of Y". Leave a 2" space. Rule horizontal lines at these marks to create panels.

3 Trace diagonal lines on the center panel to find the center point. Mark vertical and horizontal lines through the center point.

4 Using a pencil on a string as a compass, take a radius of the distance half the width of a panel. Set the pencil on the center bottom of the small top panel. Pin the string on the vertical and with the set radius below, draw an arc as shown in the diagram, left.

5 Keeping the center of the circle the same throughout, draw another arc with a radius 1" longer than the first. Increase the radius by 2" for an arc that abuts the base of the small top panel on either side. Increase the radius by 1" to draw the top arc. Repeat at the bottom of the panel.

6 Draw a border 1" inside the existing panels.

7 Mark true diagonals through the center point. Mark the lines of a four-point star, as shown, so that the side points extend two-thirds of the panel width and the vertical points extend half of the panel height, all with a common inner edge.

Color-washing

Quick, easy and inexpensive, color-washing creates translucent clouds of color. You need no special equipment—just a large paintbrush and latex paint—to add interest to walls. Vary the texture, from a subtle haze to a bold, brushy pattern, to suit your room.

Color-washing is one of the most versatile of all paint techniques. You can give a soft, broken texture to plain walls, using two coats of a single color of latex paint over a plain white base, or use two different colors to create clouds and patches with translucent depths.

You can vary the degree to which your brushstrokes show, too, so you can use color-washing to give a country-style kitchen a rustic look with random brushed patterns in a warm ocher, or soften the brushstrokes to create a sophisticated shading for an elegant dining room or a bedroom.

The technique

The charm of color-washing comes from the fact that it does not give a complete cover. The effect is an imitation of a traditional technique that used distemper to give a clouded, partial covering of color—but distemper is seldom if ever used today, and modern paints are developed to give as solid a covering of color as possible.

To produce this washy effect, you need to dilute the paint until it is thin and runny. One part paint to five parts water will give a good consistency, allowing the background color to show through. This background color can be plain

PHOTOGRAPHY BY LIZZIE ORME

white or a similar pale shade to blend with your room scheme. It is inadvisable to color-wash over a base color that is darker than the wash—the effect would be overpowered by the background and would almost disappear.

Getting started

The best base for color-washing in diluted latex paint is a satin or mid-sheen finish. Although this is water-based, it has a slight sheen, which makes it easier to brush the color wash over the surface rather than over a completely flat latex paint. Before you start, paint your room throughout in your chosen background color, making sure it is completely dry before you color-wash over it.

When you mix the color wash, make enough to complete the whole room so that you do not vary the texture of the wash halfway through the job. Diluted paint goes a long way, so one quart of latex paint will be more than enough for two coats in an average-sized room. Because of its runny consistency, the color wash is liable to drip, so protect your floor with drop cloths.

Using color wash

The secret of successful color-washing is to work quickly, in long upward diagonal crosshatched brushstrokes, covering the wall in areas of about one square yard, gradually working out of this area to extend the effect. To get an even tone, do not keep re-covering the same area, as this will build up patches of strong color. If the effect of the first coat is patchy, the second one will soften the appearance. Although it is possible to color-wash with just one coat, it is worth applying two coats for a more textured finish.

Cleaning up

Water-based paint is easy to clean away with warm, soapy water—rinse out the pail and the brush until the water runs clear. As with any brush, allow your brush to dry so that the bristles remain completely straight.

1 Prepare the walls

● Check the walls to see that they are sound—fill any cracks in plaster and sand down, or restick any curling edges of wallpaper. Clean the walls to remove any traces of dirt or grease, using an all-purpose cleaner or a warm detergent solution. Rinse with fresh water and allow to dry.

● If the base color differs from the baseboard or window frames, shield these areas with masking tape. Apply the base color with a roller and finish off the edges and corners with a brush. Allow to dry for 2–4 hours, depending on the temperature. Pour the latex paint for color-washing into a large plastic pail.

2 First coat of color

● Measure out cold water into the paint in the pail in a proportion of about 5 parts water to 1 part latex paint, depending on the thickness of the paint. Always add the water to the paint, never the other way around.

● For the first coat of color wash, start in the top left corner of a wall, making upward diagonal brushstrokes up to 1½' long. Do not pick up too much wash mixture on the brush at a time, or it will drip. The mixture should leave streaky, grainy bristle marks with each stroke of the brush.

PHOTOGRAPHY BY LIZZIE ORME

E·Q·U·I·P·M·E·N·T

YOU WILL NEED:
● All-purpose cleaner or detergent solution
● 2½ quarts satin-finish latex paint in white
● I quart latex paint in color-wash color
● 2 quarts clear matte acrylic varnish
● 4" paintbrush
● Paint roller and tray
● Large plastic pail●
Cloths and a sponge
● Scissors
The above quantities are sufficient for a 12' x 15' room

3 Crosshatched strokes

● Work outward from an area about 1 square yard in size, crisscrossing the strokes as you go. Lift the brush lightly at the end of each stroke to make a feathery, broken edge. As you complete one area, continue brushing diagonally outward to start breaking into the unwashed wall area. Do not keep working over an area that looks patchy, as this will simply build up areas of deeper color. It does not matter if the first coat appears to be very patchy, as you can adjust this with the second coat of color wash when the first coat has dried.

HELP FILE

BLOTCHES
The more color-washing you do, the easier it is to get just the right level of texture and cover. If you find that your first attempts are blotchy, use a damp sponge to blend in the hard edges and to disperse or lift off thicker areas of paint. It is easy to correct a patchy appearance without adding more paint.

CONSISTENCY
If you find that the color-wash mixture is not going on smoothly, dilute it with a little more water—it is always easy to dilute but not to thicken, so add extra water slowly.

SURFACES
Color-washing gives a random, textured finish that is ideal for disguising uneven walls. It is also suitable for plain or rough plaster finishes, cork tiles on walls, curved walls, laminated surfaces, glass or metal. Make sure you use a primer appropriate to the surface and paint over it in a water-based satin-finish paint.

DRYING TIME
Undiluted latex paint takes two to four hours to dry, but because a color wash contains so much water, it dries even more quickly. Allow two to three hours for the color wash to dry between coats.

4 Even out the edges

● Before the first coat dries, use a slightly damp paintbrush to soften any hard lines. Brush gently in the same direction as the brushstrokes.

5 Remove the dribbles

● Because the color wash is so dilute and runny, it may begin to dribble down the wall where it is applied most thickly. Use a soft cloth to remove the drips, working upward in the same direction as the brushstrokes that the wash is running over. When you have softened the edges and made sure there are no dribbles to spoil the effect, allow the color-washed area to dry for 2–3 hours.

The charm of color-washing comes from the random, brushy appearance of the finish. This makes the technique unsuitable for walls covered with lumpy paper that conceals crumbling plaster. The lumpy texture of such walls would break up and drag the brushstrokes, collecting uneven drops of paint that would spoil the overall appearance.

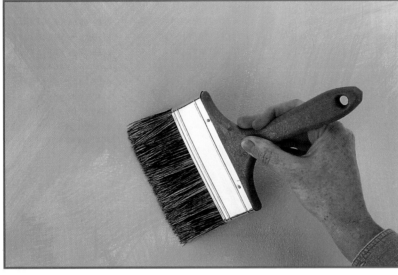

6 Second coat of color wash

● When the first coat is dry, start again, working over the existing layer, still crossing the upward diagonal brushstrokes and trying not to brush in the same direction on the second coat as on the first. Wipe away dribbles and soften the edges with a damp brush, as before.

7 Bare patches

● Stand back from the wall when you have finished to see if there are any bare areas that stand out.
● Dip a piece of sponge in a little of the color wash, dab off the excess on a piece of scrap paper, then fill in the spaces, using a light wiping action.

8 Varnishing

● When the walls are completely dry, protect the color-washed areas with a coat of clear acrylic varnish. Apply this using a wide brush in quick vertical strokes. Take care not to overwork, as this will start to lift off the color wash.

Two-color washing

1 First color

- Prepare the walls as in step 1 on page 157 and paint with white satin-finish latex paint. Allow to dry for 2–4 hours.
- Using diluted yellow latex paint, color-wash over the base following steps 2 to 4, left. Work outward in areas of about 1 square yard, using upward diagonal strokes up to 1½' long.

2 Soften the brush marks

- Before the color-washing is dry, take a clean, slightly damp brush and use it to soften any hard lines at the start of the brushstrokes. Work lightly to blur the wash, brushing it in the same direction as the brushstrokes.

3 **Wipe away dribbles**

● If dribbles of wash run off your brush or collect and start to run down the wall, use a clean cloth to wipe the excess away in the direction of the brushstrokes below the dribble of paint. Allow the first coat to dry completely.

4 **Orange color wash**

● Dilute orange latex paint with water in proportions of 1 to 5, respectively. Color-wash over the yellow paint in upward diagonal strokes, crisscrossing each other. The second color will create a translucent shading as it covers some areas that have not been covered, other areas that have one covering of yellow and places where yellow strokes cross.

5 **Soften the second color**

● Use a damp brush, as in step 2 on page 159, to soften the beginnings of the brushstrokes. Remove any dribbles of paint with a cloth, taking care not to wipe away any of the yellow color wash below.

6 **Fill in gaps**

● Take an overall look at each wall to see if there are any areas without sufficient cover. Dip a sponge in the yellow or orange color wash, dab off the excess on paper, then fill in any bare patches using a diagonal wiping movement. Allow to dry completely, then protect with clear varnish, as in step 8 on page 158.

TIPS

CORNERS
Use a little color wash to even out the effect in the angles of corners of areas you cannot reach with a large brush.

ALTERNATIVES
Instead of diluted latex paint, use a commercially prepared color wash, available from decorator's stores. This needs only one coat, and because the color is carried in a glaze rather than a latex paint, it stays "open" and workable for a longer period of time. Follow the manufacturer's instructions, and varnish when dry.

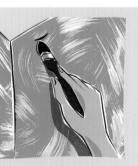

LOOSE HAIRS
If you find that your color-washing brush has shed hairs on the wall, use a completely clean, dry brush to prod one end of the hair off the wall so that you can remove it.

Liming
ON WOOD

Liming brings out the natural beauty of open-grained wood. Used with a colored stain, liming can rejuvenate the most humble piece of furniture and add a touch of country charm—it is a perfect way to transform a flea-market find.

Liming has been used for centuries to enhance and bring out the beauty of wooden surfaces, from furniture to panels, doors and walls. The traditional method used caustic lime, rubbed into the open grain of stained wood—nowadays an easy-to-use noncaustic paste is available. When this has dried, you remove the excess with steel wool; it is the lime paste, which remains embedded in the grain, that gives liming its characteristic chalky look. Hardwoods with an open grain, such as oak, ash and chestnut, are the most suitable for liming, but you could also use pine that has been scrubbed very vigorously with a wire brush to open the grain.

Liming can transform any piece of furniture, giving it a bleached, rustic look—so take this into consideration when planning the overall style of your room and furnishings. For instance, you could use liming to coordinate a set of unmatched wooden chairs. Old, dark Victorian pieces or heavy early 20th century pieces can be wonderfully transformed to look lighter and more modern.

show through the liming in a softened shade. If your wood is marked, a coat of paint is ideal to disguise it. If you think that a large stain is likely to show through, use a little wood bleach, according to the manufacturer's instructions, or dilute household bleach with water and dab it over the stain. Rinse thoroughly after applying.

Liming can be messy, so cover your hair and wear old clothes, a face mask, goggles and heavy rubber gloves. Work outdoors but not in direct sunlight, or in an area with good ventilation.

BEFORE

A pretty but heavy-looking console is an ideal candidate for the softening technique of liming.

The technique

The key to a perfect finish is the way you prepare the surface. The first step is to strip the existing finish back to the bare wood, then to open the grain with a wire brush. You can choose whether or not you color the wood before you lime it. Use a water-based wood wash or latex paint—this will

YOU WILL NEED:

- Paint stripper
- Water-based wood wash or latex paint
- Liming paste, liming wax or a pale antiquing glaze
- Shellac
- Flat or clear varnish
- Paint thinner
- Denatured alcohol
- Small paintbrushes
- Fine- and medium-grade sandpaper
- Plastic drop cloth
- Rubber gloves
- Goggles
- Mask
- Paint scraper
- Steel wool
- Lint-free cloths
- Household sponge
- Wire brush
- Scrubbing brush
- Paint pail

1 Apply paint stripper

● Remove the drawer handles and place drawers on a drop cloth or newspaper. Make sure that your work area is well ventilated as paint stripper fumes are toxic. Wearing protective rubber gloves, goggles and a mask, brush paint stripper thickly over the wood, covering the surface. Let stand for several minutes to start working.

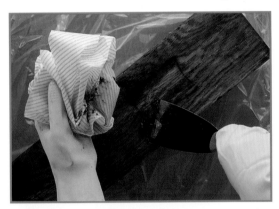

2 Remove the stripper

● As the finish starts to bubble, scrape it off using a paint scraper, using long strokes along the grain of the wood. Use steel wool to clear rounded areas and corners. The paler you can get the wood, the better it will take the stain. If the varnish is very old or thick, you may need to repeat with more paint stripper.

3 Clean the surface

● Wipe the whole surface of the wood with a cloth, according to manufacturer's instructions, to remove all traces of the paint stripper. Repeat, as necessary, to remove all the paint stripper.

4 Sponge with water

● Sponge the wood with cold water to soften the grain and to prepare the wood surface for opening with the wire brush. Use plenty of water so that it soaks in and leaves the wood slightly damp.

It is important to remove all traces of previous coats of varnish, polish or wax before you start liming on a piece of furniture. If you are starting with unfinished wood, you can omit the steps for paint stripping and begin with step 4, which prepares the wood for being scrubbed to open up the grain.

● This oak dresser was painted with brick red wood wash before being treated with the lime paste. The liming has lightened the overall color to a dusky rose, giving it a gentle, rustic and fashionable look.

5 Opening the grain

● Working in the direction of the grain, scrub firmly over the wood surface with a wire brush. If you work across the grain, you will score the wood, and this will show when the wood is limed. Use firm pressure — the more you open the grain, the more dramatic the finished effect will be — about ½₂″ depth should be sufficient.

6 Cleaning the wire brush

● You may need to clean the brush as you work. Rub it vigorously against a lint-free cloth until all bits of wood grain are removed. Wipe over the surface of the wood occasionally as you work.

7 Sand the surface

● The action of the wire brush will rough up the surface, so smooth it again by sanding lightly with medium- and then fine-grade sandpaper.

8 Remove the sanding dust

● The sanding dust will clog up the grain of the wood if left on the surface. Scrub the grain clean with a household scrubbing brush to remove all sanding particles and wood dust.

9 Dilute the wood wash

● Dilute the wood wash or latex paint with water to the consistency of heavy cream. If it is not diluted, the wood wash covers like opaque paint. Do not dilute it too much, or the color may be too weak after rubbing off the liming paste.

10 Apply the wood wash

● Brush the surface of the wood with the diluted wood wash. If necessary, allow to dry, then repeat to give a good depth of color. Remember that the liming process will lighten the finish considerably. Allow to dry—as the wash is more dilute than latex paint, this will take 2–3 hours.

11 Apply the liming paste

● Using a small brush, apply liming paste over the dry surface. Work the thick paste well into the grain, both with and across it, but avoid over-covering the wood—it will only make more dust when you come to rub it back later.

SEAN ELLIS

12 Rub off the liming paste

● When the liming paste is dry, it has a soft, powdery consistency. Using a cloth or medium- to fine-grade steel wool, rub it off at first in a circular motion, then in strokes in the direction of the grain. This is quite a long and messy job— and if you have applied the paste too thickly, it will produce an enormous amount of dust. Take care not to rub off the wood wash down to the wood, especially around corners and edges. Continue rubbing until the liming paste is left only in the open grain. Replace the cloth or steel wool whenever it becomes saturated with paste.

13 Buff the surface

● Buff the surface of the wood with a cloth to clear away any excess liming paste.

14 Seal with shellac

● It is important to seal the surface to protect the liming and to prevent discoloration or damage to the finish. With a paintbrush, apply a thinned coat of shellac. Apply sparingly, making sure there are no dribbles as these will dry to a sludgy brown. Allow to dry for about 1 hour. Clean the shellac brush thoroughly with denatured alcohol.

15 Sand the surface

● Lightly sand the surface of the wood with a piece of fine-grade sandpaper. This will smooth the surface and prepare it for the varnish.

16 Seal with varnish

● Finally, apply the varnish sparingly over the sanded surface with a small paintbrush, using long, gliding strokes. Keep the coat smooth and even to avoid any built-up areas of varnish. Allow to dry overnight.

Ideas

Liming produces a soft effect, ideal for a rustic kitchen, a pastel bedroom—or any room where you want to add a touch of gentle charm.

BOOKENDS
Smaller items, such as these ash bookends, may be limed to add an elegant, textured touch to a shelf or mantelpiece. A base of dark green has faded to a warm sage green through the liming process—a perfect complement to the natural-looking, textured-paper covers of the books.

LIMED CHAIR
This plain, straight-backed wooden chair was colored with dark blue wood wash before being limed—the result is a soft, powdery blue shade that will blend well with other limed pieces. The seat is covered in a complementary fabric of dusky blue and soft gold.

SEAN ELLIS

Country flavor

The dusted, pastel quality of colors produced by the liming technique gives wood a light, country flavor. You can emphasize this look by teaming limed furniture with cottage style or French provincial accessories and fabrics. Wall colors should also harmonize, as well as carpets and fixtures. Turn a favorite patchwork quilt or wall hanging into a focal point for a bedroom or family room by choosing accent colors from it for liming and for coordinating soft furnishings. Complete the look with a dried flower arrangement set on top of a limed bedside table, or a china pitcher filled with fresh flowers on a limed dresser.

Kitchens

Liming is an excellent way to give your kitchen a new lease on life. You can refurbish tired wooden cabinet doors in the same way as any other piece of furniture—simply remove the doors from their hinges and carry out work as before. If the wood is undamaged and attractive, consider leaving in its natural state without coloring it before liming. A limed Welsh dresser, with a complementary china display, can make a stylish focal point for a room. Rustic wrought-iron kitchen utensils, hooks and baskets can complete the look.

Color variations

Wood wash—a water-based paint very similar to latex—is available at specialty paint shops and is available in colors ideal for liming. The best colors are those that blend with the natural tones of the wood, including shades of green, blue, maroon and black. Bear in mind that all colors will be slightly yellowed when applied to the wood—for example, blue will have a slightly green tinge. Darker shades work best—if you start out with a dark blue wood wash, the end result will be the color of faded blue jeans.

Baltic blue

Soft black

Sea blue

Conifer

Gitane

Midnight blue

Natural

Gustavian green

Olive

Mulberry

PHOTOGRAPHY BY SEAN ELLIS

STEEL WOOL
If you choose to use steel wool as opposed to a cloth for removing the liming paste, take care that you do not overdo it and rub right back through the wood wash to the bare wood. Be particularly gentle around corners,

edges and delicate moldings. Variations in color add to the natural effect, but too much bare wood will spoil the effect. Try fine-grade sandpaper to rub down smaller areas.

REMOVING FRENCH POLISH
If the piece of furniture you want to lime has a finish of French polish, remove it with a cloth soaked in denatured alcohol.

HEART GRAIN
Scrub the grain open more firmly on areas with heart graining to create a more dramatic finished effect.

TRICKY CORNERS
Some corners are difficult to get into in order to remove the liming paste evenly. To avoid taking off the wood wash as well, use an old toothbrush to work into odd angles and moldings.

Stamping

Put the humble potato to decorative use to create a stylized tree mural. The technique is inexpensive, simple and needs very little planning—it's a quick and easy way of creating your own unique wall design.

YOU WILL NEED:

- **8 oz flat water-based paint in each of six colors—peach, apricot, three shades of green, brown**
- **1 1/2 quarts flat latex paint in background color (we used cream)**
- **Small paintbrush**
- **Small artist's brush**
- **Two large potatoes**
- **One unripe pear**
- **Plumb line**
- **Pencil with eraser**
- **Scissors**
- **String**
- **Ruler**
- **Pushpin**
- **Cutting board**
- **Kitchen utility knife**
- **Felt-tipped pen**
- **Craft knife**
- **Piece of glass with edges taped or an acrylic board**
- **Paper towels**
- **Cloth**

You need nothing more costly than a few potatoes and some firm fruit to create charming stylized images on walls, accessories or furniture. A step up from stamping in regular, uniform patterns, this simple technique requires very little planning and excluding necessary drying time between colors, is very quick to complete. Experiment with different designs—abstract or geometric shapes and different sizes—the effect is as versatile as simple stenciling.

Materials

It is important when stamping an item to have a smooth, flat surface, both on the stamp and on the item on which you are doing the stamping. A potato stamp will not produce a good stamped image on a rough wall—you would need to cut a stamp out of firm sponge to make a good stamped impression on such a surface. Similarly, this type of stamping would be unsuitable for curved surfaces, such as pottery.

The technique uses very little paint—a small can of paint in each color is plenty to complete a single-motif design such as the pear tree. You will only need a couple of stamps for each shape too—the firm surface of a potato or an unripe pear will last throughout a small project, so there is no need to spend a lot of time cutting stamps.

Safety first

Always use a cutting board for cutting the potatoes for your stamps—it is safer than slicing them in your hand, and you are also more likely to get a completely flat surface. When trimming away the area around the stamp, use a sharp craft knife and cut downward onto a flat surface, keeping your fingers away from the knife blade.

1 Prepare the background

● Suspend a plumb line where you want to position the tree. Make regular pencil marks down the line, extending beyond the height of the trunk as a guide for stamping the foliage.

2 Plan the tree shape

● Mark the top of the trunk and decide on the radius of the foliage area. Attach a pencil to a piece of string, then measure back along the string the distance of the radius. Pin it on the extended pencil line so that the pencil abuts the top of the trunk and draw in the circle.

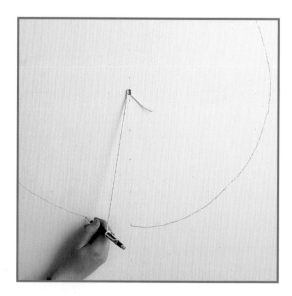

3 **Draw the shapes**

● Cut two potatoes in half; using the felt-tipped pen, draw a rectangle on one half to use as a segment of the trunk. On the other half, draw a leaf shape. Draw a slightly different leaf shape on one half of the second potato.

4 **Cut out the stamps**

● Cut the pear in half. Use the craft knife to cut an outline about ½" deep around the marked shapes, then carefully trim away the potato around the shapes to leave clean edges on the rectangle and leaf shapes.

5 **Prepare the paint**

● Using the glass as a palette, spread a little of the apricot and peach paints over the surface, overlapping each paint slightly to blend the colors.

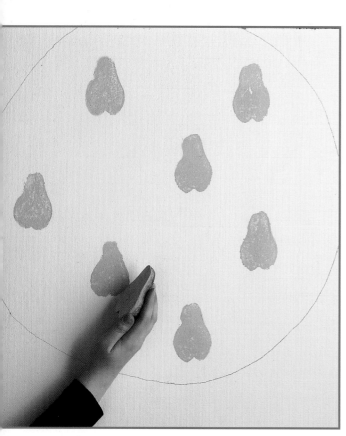

6 Stamp the pears

● Dab a pear half into the paint, picking up a little of both colors. Dab off excess paint on a paper towel, then stamp pear shapes at intervals within the marked pencil circle. Reload with paint as and when necessary.

8 Add the trunk

● Load the rectangle stamp with a little brown paint. Starting at top and working down, stamp over the pencil marks, leaving a slight space between prints, as shown.

Use a nonserrated knife edge to halve the potatoes and pears completely flat, or the imprint will not come out cleanly or completely when used.

7 Stamp the leaves

● Clean the glass and spread a little of the first shade of green over it. Load the leaf stamp with green as above and stamp random leaves within the circle. Allow to dry for 2 hours; repeat, using the other two greens and overlapping the prints for a realistic look.

9 Prepare the surface

● When all the stamping is dry, use a small artist's brush and the background color to touch up any smudged edges. Erase the pencil lines, if necessary, and touch up with the background paint.

STEVE DALTON

■ There is no need to use a new leaf stamp for each green—slight blending of colors enhances the effect.

■ For speed, apply the paint to the stamps using a small paintbrush—this allows for deliberate blending on the stamp. Remember to wipe off the excess as before.

■ If your pears are not pear-shaped enough, trim them with a small knife to get the effect you want.

■ If the paint tends to collect around the edges of the stamp as you load it, wipe around the edge of it with a paper towel to give a cleaner print.

Two-color stamping

As you get more adept, try two-color stamping with a more complicated shape, such as a strawberry (above). Cut out grooves to separate two-color areas and small spots to represent pips—make sure these are deep enough and not full of paint when you stamp, or they will not show up. Apply two colors of paint to the stamp, spreading the paint carefully, using a small paintbrush or a large artist's brush.

Use stamped motifs to coordinate accessories such as pillow covers or table linen. Follow exactly the same procedure but use fabric paints. (You will need to wash new fabric to remove the sizing before you stamp on it.) The print on the right was created using half an apple (or you could use an apple shape cut from a large potato) and potato-stamp leaves. The background is a simple combination of random squares in two colors and scattered smaller squares in a contrasting shade.

Ideal for decorating small pieces of furniture or accessories, this simple glaze technique offers endless possibilities of patterns and color combinations—using easy-to-clean acrylic glazing medium and a handful of cork stoppers.

Cork rolling

Based on the traditional technique of vinegar painting, cork rolling offers the same versatility of pattern, texture and color —with none of the problems.

The basic technique of vinegar painting used a homemade glaze brushed over a background of plain color. You would then use a cork stopper or a wad of putty or strips of modeling clay to make prints and patterns in the mixture while it was still tacky. In practice, this technique has distinct drawbacks, not the least the lingering smell of vinegar and the extremely long drying time of the improvised glaze. However, today's acrylic glazing medium has an ideal texture in which to print patterns and it dries in a matter of hours with no noticeable smell.

Materials

As a base for cork rolling, you need acrylic paint or satin-finish latex—both of which dry to a nonporous sheen, which is ideal as a background for the acrylic glazing medium—and artist's acrylic colors with which to tint the medium. For the actual rolling, you need a supply of cork stoppers; for some more experimental effects, try strips of modeling clay, pencils or soft putty—anything that will create an interesting impression when pressed or rolled over the wet glaze.

Surfaces

You can apply the cork rolling technique to any surface that can be painted, provided it is properly prepared. The only consideration apart from this is to ensure that the surface is fairly smooth. The effect of cork rolling or dabbing imprints into glaze with putty or modeling clay would be spoiled by a texture that is already rough or broken—so avoid using the technique over very craggy pottery pieces or heavily carved, detailed surfaces.

Because acrylic glazing medium is water-based, the surface is washable, but it is advisable to give a protective coating of acrylic spray varnish to items that are likely to be subjected to any wear and tear. Also, because it is water-based, you can clean your brushes and corks in warm soapy water so that they can be used again.

PHOTOGRAPHY BY ADRIAN TAYLOR

1 Prepare the surface

● Sand the surface with medium-grade sandpaper so that paint will adhere well. Wipe with a damp cloth to remove any sanding dust. (If starting with unfinished wood, rub down and treat with water-based primer as a base for the paint.)

4 Colour the glaze

● Pour a little acrylic glazing medium into a small container or paint pail and squeeze in a little artist's acrylic color. Using a mixing stick or a plastic spoon, mix well to make a smooth, evenly colored paste. Do not dilute the medium— when applied over the base coat, the mixture should be thick and sticky.

2 Apply the base coat

● Apply a coat of the base color to the prepared surface. On a laminated door such as this, finish the whole door with vertical brushstrokes. If working on a wooden door, finish the side rails, panel and recessed panel edges with vertical strokes and the top and bottom stiles with horizontal brushstrokes—working in the direction of the grain. Allow to dry for 2–4 hours.

3 Prepare the base

● To make an extra-smooth surface on which to roll the cork, sand the base coat with fine-grade sandpaper. On wooden surfaces, work in the direction of the grain. Wipe with a tack cloth to remove all traces of dust.

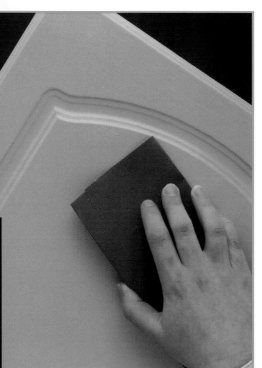

6 Cork rolling

● Holding the cork on its side between your index fingers and thumbs, roll it over the wet glaze in a series of continuous abutting lines, wiping it clean with a cloth between rows (see inset). If you make a mistake, brush the glaze over and start again.

5 Glazing

● Apply the glazing mixture with a paintbrush. Do not make the covering too thick, because the cork stopper will redistribute the glaze when it is rolled through it. Because the glaze will start to dry immediately, work in stages, starting with the central panel, using even, vertical brushstrokes.

7 Glaze the door frame

● Apply the glazing mixture over the frame of the door, working in vertical brushstrokes to match the center panel. It does not matter if you brush glaze into the recess around the panel—this can be wiped off later. Roll the cork in abutting vertical strips, as in step 6.

8 Wipe off excess glaze

● Moisten a cloth with water and with it wrapped around your index finger, draw it around the recess to remove any excess glaze and to give a clean edge around the panel.

9 Protect with varnish

● Although glazing medium dries to an impermeable finish, you may want to give added protection of a coat of acrylic varnish. Apply over the dry glaze in vertical brushstrokes.

HELP FILE

MODELING CLAY
To use modeling clay for rolling, break off four strips together; cut into a 3" to 4¾" length. Still keeping them in a square shape, press to mold them together. Roll this over the glaze for a ridged effect.

MIXING COLORS
When adding the acrylic color to the glazing medium, use a sturdy mixing stick and stir in a figure eight. This will help to disperse the color more quickly and evenly. Remember that the tinted glazing medium must be mixed thoroughly before you use it.

CORK STOPPERS
Cork stoppers that have been cut in a solid piece from the bark of a tree give a different pattern from those that are made from reconstituted cork. Solid cork stoppers give a more open pattern, while reconstituted cork stoppers produce a more defined surface texture. Collect an assortment of cork stoppers and experiment with them to see the different patterns they produce.

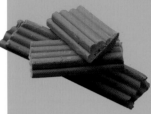

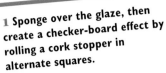

1 Sponge over the glaze, then create a checker-board effect by rolling a cork stopper in alternate squares.

Pattern guide

2 Roll alternate squares with a four-sided strip of modeling clay—stamp the spaces with the base of the cork stopper.

3 Rock the cork stopper backward and forward, building up a pattern by changing directions.

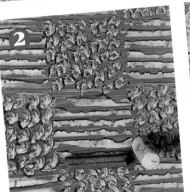

Plant pot

● Cork rolling is ideal for decorating a smooth, curved surface, such as an earthenware pot, adding an extra dimension to the plain surface. Be sure to keep your cork stopper wiped clean as you work.

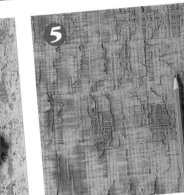

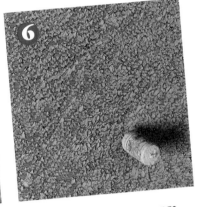

4 For a striped pattern, sponge the glaze to disperse the brushstrokes, then roll the cork stopper over the glaze in evenly spaced lines, leaving sponged areas in between.

5 Roll a six-sided pencil over the wet glaze to create an effect like rain on a windowpane. Overlap the pencil lines slightly as you work.

6 For a dappled pattern, use the base of the cork stopper and dab it randomly all over the wet glaze.

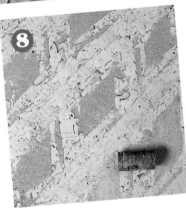

7 Press together a four-sided strip of modeling clay and roll it in alternating vertical and horizontal squares over the glaze.

8 Sponge the glaze to disperse the brushstrokes. Roll the cork stopper over the glaze in evenly spaced vertical lines, then in diagonal lines.

9 Roll the cork stopper over the glaze in one direction. Repeat in abutting rows, wiping the cork clean frequently.

Aging effects

Brand new furniture and sparkling paintwork are crisp and fresh—but they lack today's fashionable look of gentle aging. Here's how to recreate that special, time-softened elegance.

YOU WILL NEED:

- Mid-sheen oil-based paint in terra-cotta
- Flat latex paint in peachy pink
- Fleur de lys stencil
- Gold water-based paint
- Large paintbrush
- Medium-sized paintbrush
- Household sponge or foam sponge
- Paint thinner
- Denatured alcohol
- Rubber gloves
- Lint-free cloth
- Pencil
- Ruler
- Tape measure
- Cutting mat
- Stencil acetate
- Craft knife
- Set square
- Masking tape
- Scissors
- Plain white paper
- Plastic plates
- Red felt-tipped pen

Antique furniture, old walls and worn paintwork have a charming mellow quality, with no two pieces of old furniture ever the same. But collecting antique furniture can be expensive, and new pieces can take years to achieve that timeworn look. You can speed up the aging process, using simple techniques to add years to new furniture or walls.

The techniques

Both techniques work on the principle of building up layers of paint and rubbing them back. On the wall, a layer of latex paint is painted over a coat of mid-sheen oil-based paint and then rubbed back with denatured alcohol. The finished effect looks like distemper—a traditional paint finish used before the advent of modern paints, which had a soft, chalky texture.

For furniture, use a different type of distressing, building up layers of color as for the wall technique but using steel wool to rub back the top coat of paint to reveal the second color underneath.

Subtle distressing

The secret with aging is not to overdo it. Because your layers of paint are planned, you can choose colors that look good together—as opposed to the color combination being the accident of time. You can choose where you add the distressed look too. When you rub candle wax over a piece of furniture, you will find that you naturally get more coverage on the areas that stand out—corners, edges or round moldings—which creates an authentic worn appearance.

1 Apply base coat

- Make sure that the wall is clean and dry; then, using the large paintbrush, apply a coat of terra-cotta oil-based paint. Allow to dry for up to 16 hours, depending on the room temperature. Clean the brush with paint thinner.

The fumes from denatured alcohol can be harmful if inhaled, so when using it, always work in a well-ventilated room. Also, because it is highly flammable, keep it away from open flames of any kind.

2 Apply the latex

● Using crisscross strokes, brush the pink paint sparingly all over the walls, including any trim or molding. It doesn't matter if patches of the base color show through—this enhances the effect. Allow to dry.

3 Rubbing back

● Wearing rubber gloves, soak the cloth in denatured alcohol and rub it all over the dry paintwork, taking off patches of the pink paint to reveal the terra-cotta paint below.

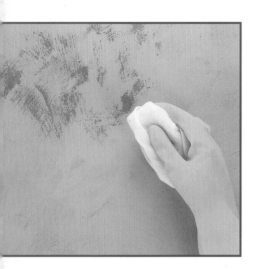

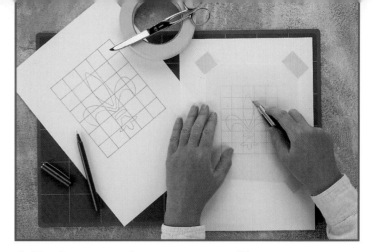

4 Reduce and cut a stencil

● To make a small fleur-de-lis motif, trace the outline from the stencil, reduce the image by about one-third either by using a paper grid or by photocopying. Using a craft knife and a cutting mat, cut the stencil out of acetate.

5 Mark the stencil positions

● Measure points 6" up from the chair rail all around the room; if you do not have a chair rail, measure a chosen height up from the baseboard. Connect the points with a pencil and mark off intervals of about 14", according to the size of the stencil.

6 Position the stencil

● Making sure that the stencil sits straight, position it so that the point of the fleur-de-lis just meets the pencil line at one of the marked intervals.

7 Stencil the motifs

● Pour a little gold paint onto a plastic plate; using a small piece of sponge, stencil the fleur-de-lis motifs on the pencil-marked positions all around the walls.

Distressed cabinet

Distressing is one of the most effective—and simplest—ways to age furniture and paintwork.

1 Sanding and cleaning

● Sand the whole cabinet with fine-grade sandpaper and wipe clean with a damp cloth. When dry, apply a coat of charcoal flat latex paint and allow to dry for 2–4 hours.

YOU WILL NEED:

● 16 oz flat latex paint in charcoal, lime green and blue
● A small amount of latex paint or artist's acrylic paint in brown
● Chosen stencil design
● Water-based stencil paint in pink
● Water-based varnish
● Two medium-sized paintbrushes
● Dragging brush
● Household sponge or foam sponge
● Fine-grade sandpaper
● Wax candle
● Medium-grade steel wool
● Tack cloth
● Stencil acetate
● Cutting mat
● Craft knife
● Scissors
● Masking tape
● Plastic plate
● Mixing bowl
● Mixing sticks or spoons

The secret of this type of distressing is the use of candle wax. First give your piece of furniture a base coat in the color that you want to see showing through the top coat, then rub a wax candle over the whole piece in areas that tend to take the most wear and tear over the years, such as on the corners and edges. Now when you paint the piece in your main color, the paint will not adhere to the waxed areas and it will come away easily when rubbed back, revealing the first color beneath.

To add interest to the finish, use a stencil to decorate the doors of the cabinet, then age the surface with a dulling mixture. If you prefer, you can always distress stenciled areas, making sure that the paint is completely dry, by rubbing the surface lightly with fine-grade steel wool.

Before

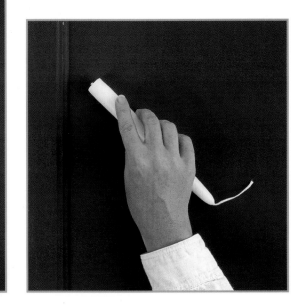

2 Rub with candle wax

● Using the candle on its side, rub all over the cabinet, paying special attention to the edges and corners. If you look at the cabinet in the right light, you should be able to see where the wax is and add more where necessary.

3 The second coat

● Apply an even coat of lime green paint, brushing the paint in a vertical direction on the doors and with the grain of the wood on the rest of the cupboard.

4 Rub back the paint

● Using the steel wool, rub the paint in the direction of the wood grain underneath. Where there is wax underneath, the paint will come away easily to reveal the charcoal color beneath.

! Avoid rubbing steel wool against the grain of the wood and the direction of the brushstrokes, as this will create an ugly, scratchy effect instead of a smooth distressing.

5 Building layers

● Rub again with wax; then, using the dragging brush and very little blue paint, drag over the top. When dry, rub back and repeat steps 4 and 5 on just the doors.

6 Cut the stencil

● If you are cutting your own stencil, attach the design to a cutting mat with masking tape. Secure the acetate over the top and cut, using a craft knife.

7 Stencil the design

● Make sure the stencil is positioned symmetrically on the top of the door, then secure it in place with masking tape. Stencil in pink using a piece of sponge, then repeat on the other door. When dry, rub the doors over lightly with candle wax.

9 Added aging

● Using the dragging brush, lightly brush the blue-brown mixture over the cabinet doors, keeping the strokes in a vertical direction. This adds a dull patina, which enhances the aged appearance.

8 Blending colors

● Pour a little blue paint into a small container and blend in a bit of brown latex paint or artist's oil color. Mix well and, if still quite thick, dilute with a little water.

Color guide

Vary colors to give an effect as subtle or as emphatic as you wish.

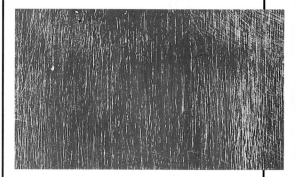

■ Start with a base of primrose yellow paint and when dry, rub over randomly with candle wax, leaving some areas untouched for a patchy effect. Apply a coat of dark blue, allow to dry, then rub back to reveal patches of color.

■ Create a look like old wood, using a base of pale beige; then, after applying patches of candle wax, add a top coat of dull brown, watered down with half again as much water. When this is rubbed back, it will leave a more streaky effect.

■ For very light distressing—especially with two strongly contrasting colors—apply wax lightly in vertical strokes using just one edge of the candle. When rubbed back, a white background will show through in small flecks.

BUYER'S GUIDE

Stenciling supplies and painting supplies are readily available at crafts shops, art supply stores and paint stores. Interior latex and oil-based paints and general painting supplies are carried by paint stores, home-improvement centers and hardware stores. Listed below is a sampling of mail-order sources that carry harder-to-find supplies and manufacturers to call for information.

Adele Bishop
P. O. Box 3349
Kinston, NC 28502
800-334-4186

Catalog $4.00, refundable with first order. Stencil paints, stencil supplies, stencil kits.

Binney & Smith, Inc.
1100 Church Lane
P. O. Box 431
Easton, PA 18044-0431

800-272-9652.
Call for nearest local retailer. Acrylic enamel paint, artist's oil paints, acrylic paints.

Constantine's
2050 Eastchester Road
Bronx, NY 10461
800-223-8087

Free woodworker's catalog. Plaster moldings and rosettes, antique-restoration supplies.

Craft King Discount Craft Supply
P. O. Box 90637
Lakeland, FL 33804
800-769-9494

Free catalog.
Arts and crafts supplies.

Delta Technical Coatings, Inc.
2550 Pellissier Place
Whittier, CA 90601
800-423-4135.

Call for nearest local retailer. Paint supplies, including stencil paint, acrylic paint, ceramic and tile paint, crackle medium, stains, finishes.

Dick Blick
P. O. Box 1267
Galesburg, IL 61402-1267
800-447-8192

Catalog $5.00, refundable with first order. Art supplies, including powder pigments, airbrush markers, brushes, crackle medium, varnishes, fabric crayons, acrylic paints, ceramic paints, acrylic mediums, artist's oil colors, adhesives

Duncan Enterprises
5673 E. Shields Avenue
Fresno, CA 93727
209-291-4444.

Call for nearest local retailer. Aleene's acrylic paints and mediums.

Janovic/Plaza
30-35 Thomson Avenue
Long Island City, NY 11101
800-772-4381

Catalog $4.95.
Specialty decorating supplies, including paints, graining combs, graining rollers, varnishes, sealers, glazing liquids, brushes.

McCloskey Varnish Company
1191 South Wheeling Road
Wheeling, IL 60090
800-345-4530.

Call for nearest local retailer. Glazing liquids, wood stains.

Paint Effects
2426 Fillmore Street
San Francisco, CA 94115
415-292-7780

Web page:
www.painteffects.com
Formerly known as Paint Magic.
Call or use web page to order.
Decorative painting and faux-finishing supplies, including liming wax, pre-mixed glazes, crackle glazes, color-washing supplies, wood-washing supplies.

Pearl Paint
308 Canal Street
New York, NY 10013-2572
Attn: Catalog Dept.
800-221-6845

Catalog $1.00. Fine art, craft and graphic discount supplies, including artist's oil colors, powder pigments, acrylic paints, faux finish glazes, mediums, brushes, adhesives.

Plaid Enterprises, Inc.
1649 International Ct.
P. O. 7600
Norcross, GA 30091-7600
800-842-4197.

Call for nearest local retailer. Stencil supplies, acrylic paints, brushes, crackle medium, antiquing paint, glazes, graining combs.

Pottery Barn
P. O. Box 7044
San Francisco,
CA 94120-7044
800-922-5507.

Call for nearest local Decorator Store. Paint Magic kits for crackle glazing, wood-washing and color-washing are available at Pottery Barn Decorator Stores around the country.

Sax Arts & Crafts
P. O. Box 510710
New Berlin, WI 53151-0710
800-558-6696

Catalog $5.00, refunded with first order; minimum order of $10.00.
Arts and crafts supplies, including artist's oil colors, artist's acrylic colors, powder pigments, cork stoppers, stencil paint crayons, fabric crayons, brushes, mediums, palettes.

S&S Worldwide
P. O. Box 513
Colchester, CT 06415-0513
800-243-9232

Free catalog; minimum order of $25.00. General arts and crafts supplies, including child's air art gun and markers, modeling clay, fabric crayons, adhesives.

Thompson & Formby, Inc.
825 Crossover Lane
Memphis, TN 38117
800-367-6297.

Call for nearest local retailer. Wood stains, glazes, antiquing kits, sponging kits.

United Gilsonite Laboratories
P. O. Box 70
Scranton, PA 18501-0070
800-272-3235

Free brochure. Rocker-type graining tool (ZAR Graining Tool), wood stain.

INDEX